Barbara Pere...

Seasons of My Heart

Illustrated by
CARRIE PARKS

Copyright of text © 1998 by Barbara Peretti
Copyright of illustrations © 1998 by Carrie Parks

Published by J. Countryman®, a division of Thomas Nelson Inc.,
Nashville, Tennessee 37214

Project Editor—Terri Gibbs

A *J. Countryman®* Book

Designed by Garborg Design Works
Minneapolis, Minnesota

ISBN: 0-8499-5373-1

Printed and bound in the United States of America

To

Frank E. Peretti

My wonderful husband, lover, and best friend.

Thank you for twenty-six years
of wonderful married life.

You have said I am the jewel in your life.
Well, it is the light of your love that illumines me.
God created you to be the perfect setting that makes me shine.

I love you!

Contents

FOREWORD

At this season in our lives, Barb and I have been doing a lot of reflecting and reviewing. We've pulled out all the journals and appointment calendars; we've reopened old letters and paged through our photo albums. We want to recall where we've been, what we've done, what we've become, and what it all means. Only God knows *all* the answers, but we've managed to find a few, and Barb has written about them: the lessons, the insights, the experiences, and the things that really matter.

She's never written a book before, but this is *Barb* we're talking about. She never flew a plane before or knew the first thing about watercolor painting, but now she's done both and, as you will see, this gal can write. Most of our collaboration was simply the fact that we lived the story together.

When Crossway Books published *This Present Darkness* in 1986, my first novel carried this short dedication: *To Barbara Jean, wife and friend, who loved me, and waited.* The book you are holding, penned by my wife and friend, is the story that lies behind that dedication. My novels have done well and made their "big splash," but none of them could have become reality without the love that endured, the waiting that had to be, and the lovely saint who stood with me through it all. I am pleased to introduce her to you, and I know you'll like her as you get to know her through these pages.

She loved me,

    she waited,

        and I will love her always.

Frank E. Peretti

Acknowledgments

One would think that the author of an autobiographical book would simply record a succession of events from a particular beginning in history to an ending and be done with it. But as I saw this project reach beyond the limits of a simple autobiographical manuscript to a beautifully created and illustrated gift book, it dawned on me that the exquisite work you now hold would never have come about without the help of the following people:

To Jack Countryman and Kip Jordan for their kind acceptance of my manuscript and their vision to make it a beautiful book, I'm greatly appreciative—to say the least!

I applaud Terri Gibbs, Managing Editor, for her

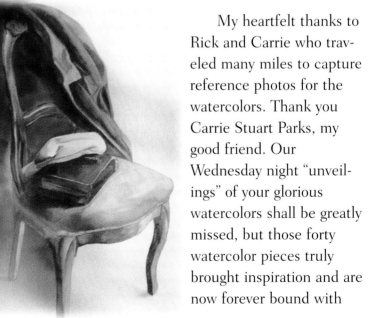

painstaking job of editing my manuscript. She has marvelously woven a beautiful tapestry of my words, Scripture, and additional thoughts. Bravo!

To all at J. Countryman who had even the slightest input in this project, I appreciate your help. I will probably never fully know all that you have done.

My heartfelt thanks to Rick and Carrie who traveled many miles to capture reference photos for the watercolors. Thank you Carrie Stuart Parks, my good friend. Our Wednesday night "unveilings" of your glorious watercolors shall be greatly missed, but those forty watercolor pieces truly brought inspiration and are now forever bound with my words in this book. You've caught our breath away!

Rick, thank you for soaking, stretching, stapling, and taping each 24-by-48-inch sheet of Arches' 140-pound paper onto plywood. Without even a murmur in my direction, you devoted hours away from crafting artwork on instrument tops and creating CD covers to meticulously penciling the lifelike drawings from which Carrie's watercolors emerged. I gratefully acknowledge your thoughtfulness and creativity on this project.

Loving gratitude goes to my husband, Frank, who not only refreshed my memory with details of our life but, as my teacher and first editor, also taught me to gather my wandering thoughts into one organized unit. Hopefully, I have achieved that and will get a good grade on this book!

Also, much thanks to the following people for their participation with the artwork: Greg Blake and Marc Cook of Bear Creek Crafters for providing antique carpentry tools for "Trusting and Waiting"; Claudia Kenyon Laskey and Silver Mountain Resort for the antique skis used for reference in "The End of a Chapter"; Donna and JB Lindsey for reference photos for "Trusting Jesus to Lead the Way"; Courtney Lindsey who modeled for "Trusting Jesus to Lead the Way"; Corrine Oberg for posing for "Faith as a Child"; Don Parks for supplying reference photos for "Little Country Church"; Laurie, Scott, and Aynslee Stuart for assisting and posing for "Little Ones to Him Belong"; Kerry and John Woods for the sheep and Great Pyrenees models for "The Beginning of Our Story" and "Timeless Treasures."

Much thanks also to Monkia Hardy for locating the words to "Little Country Church."

Finally, Frank and I shall always be indebted to our wonderful parents who raised us on God's Word and taught us to remain faithful to the Lord. We shall forever be grateful for this wealth you have passed on to us. Truly Frank and I have been spiritually blessed because of you!

Introduction

Reminiscing back through twenty-five years of marriage has given me a broader perspective of the seasons God has brought Frank and me through. I have gained a measure of assurance, knowing that if the present is not glorious, it is not that God has left us; rather, He is silently working to develop His character in our lives. As I reflect on the more difficult seasons of our married life, I am reminded of our severe winter in 1996.

October. Early frosts shriveled the bright leaves of autumn. Pumpkins had barely been plucked from our gardens when winter covered the ground with the first blanket of snow.

November. More snow fell. By Thanksgiving the green grass of summer lay buried under more than a foot of the stuff.

Christmas. We shoveled snow from beneath our windows. It was obstructing our view! I envisioned Old Man Winter hovering over us, his blue-gray, cumulus-cloud face with cheeks full of icy wind puffing blasts of winter over us without mercy. Frank and I had no sooner finished blowing snow to clear the pathway and driveway than another system arrived, dropping temperatures and visibility to zero. The rising snow gave the illusion that our house had sunk another eight inches into the ground. Old Man Winter just kept blowing. Could we hold on until spring?

Through the kitchen window I watched the cold air hovering over our valley. Wisps of warm fog rose from the river like ghostly spirits sentenced from the swirling currants into the icy prison of winter. I remembered that it was only a few months ago when had we donned sunglasses, sunscreen, and sun hats to shield ourselves from solar rays as we rafted on the river. Did we actually sit on our deck in shorts and sleeveless shirts pecking at manuscripts while beads of perspiration scribed meandering pathways down our necks?

What a contrast between the two pictures! And what a visual reminder that seasons do change.

At last, a few days in the fifties. Spring!

MARCH. *Fourteen . . . eighteen* degrees! Our promise of spring was dashed by Old Man Winter again. Yet my hope was refreshed, knowing that after every winter, spring always follows, bringing with it a sigh of relief and a much awaited interlude from winter's blast. I clung to this hope as the late March winds whistled through my windows and piled frost and snow against the panes.

Just as winter transforms into spring, so our lives are transformed from one season to the next. When Frank and I endure a difficult season, it seems an eternity. But when our days are easy, it feels like an instant. As surely as we hoped for spring in the midst of winter, so through our twenty-five years of marriage we have hoped in God to bring reprieve during seasons of unfulfilled hopes, doubts, and financial difficulties.

Daffodils still bloom after a severe frost, and the apple tree bears fruit after a season of dormancy. And the God who carefully created the daffodils and apple trees also orchestrates the seasons of our lives to fulfill His unique plan for each of us. So when our seasons change, Frank and I have learned to quiet ourselves before the Almighty and wait to hear His voice.

Barbara J. Peretti

AUGUST 1998

I was sixteen and dating the young man I planned to marry after graduation. It was a perfect time to meet Frank Peretti.

Frank had been speaking to our church youth group. He encouraged us to "sell out to Jesus," "die to self," and "commit our lives wholeheartedly to God." Frank's own commitment to serve God was certainly obvious. I respected that in him. I liked his fervent sincerity and dedication—in fact, there was more and more about him that I was beginning to like. The problem was, I didn't need another romantic relationship. The young man I was dating seemed just right for me.

Under God's nudging over the next few months, I began to question the sincerity and commitment of my life. I decided I wanted more than a mediocre walk with God. As I was reading my Bible, He impressed upon my heart Proverbs 14:12, "There is a way that seems right . . . but its end is the way of death."

CHAPTER 1
The Beginning of Our Story

Who was I to think I could direct my own course in life? It became clear that I had to give up what I felt was right and give full control of my life to God.

Once I made the decision to submit completely to God's will, life became very interesting. . .

I woke up late one morning and was tired and grumpy by the time I got to school. It was going to be a rough day. Between classes I was studying for a test (while struggling to stay awake), when a friend popped his head around the door of the classroom.

"Barb! Frank's out here in the hall!"

I looked up. "Huh?"

"Frank Peretti's here!"

Frank Peretti, I thought. *Why do I feel that's significant this morning?*

An instant later, it was as if I had been struck by lightening. I felt a surge of

warmth flow from my head all the way down my body. Tears filled my eyes. I couldn't speak or move.

Suddenly it dawned on me. *My fleece! God has answered my fleece!*

I had nearly forgotten. The night before I had been up late reading Deuteronomy eleven and felt God distinctly speaking to my heart. He told me who I was to marry and shared that if we would let Him guide our lives He would cause us to be fruitful and would care for us from the beginning of the year even to the end of the year. I remembered how Gideon had tested God's direction with a fleece of lamb's wool and decided to put out my own "fleece." I told God that if He truly wanted me to marry Frank Peretti, He would have to confirm that by having Frank show up at my school the next day . . . an extremely unlikely possibility.

Now, here he was!

> *And it shall be that if you earnestly obey My commandments which I command you today, to love the LORD your God and serve Him with all your heart and with all your soul, then I will give you the rain for your land in its season. . . .*
>
> DEUTERONOMY 11:13–14

I felt very, very small before Almighty God. I wanted to kneel down and cover my head. God was communicating with *me*! I had surrendered my all to Him, and He was giving it back with a mandate—I was to marry Frank Peretti!

One thing I knew for sure: I was *not* going to tell Frank!

Only later did I learn Frank's perspective on that day. The previous night he had received a telephone call asking him to come to school the next day to share Jesus with a friend. During the night he woke from a disturbing dream and called out to God, asking Him to send someone into his life whom he could love—someone who would love him in return.

Little did we know that our story was just beginning, . . . and God, the Master Storyteller, certainly knows how to weave a wonderful story.

To Frank and I, the love between a man and a woman is holy. In honor of this sacredness, we agreed that there would be no physical expression of our affection for each other until we had declared our love. As each day passed, we moved closer to that moment, as did our longing to share an affectionate hug or a tender kiss.

It was a June evening . . . warm as evenings go on an island in Puget Sound. Frank and I decided to take a walk before nightfall. It was a familiar course down the steep hill of Glen Acres Road, meandering through the cedar and madrona trees. Wafting up the bank from the beach, the aroma of seaweed, mussels, and wet sand was carried along with the call of seagulls. We walked but did not hold hands.

Coming to the end of the road, we sat in a small clearing overlooking Seattle. As daylight departed, the lights of the city began to glitter across the water giving the appearance of flickering fireflies.

As darkness fell we retraced our steps through the trees, down the road. When we were nearly home, Frank turned to me and asked, "How are you feeling about us, about me?" I didn't answer. Instead, I returned the question. He stopped walking and bent down to pick up a rock that he threw into the woods. He hemmed and hawed, grinding dirt into the pavement with his foot. Finally, he laid down on the road, flat on his back, and sighed, "I have something I need to read to you." He stood up and put his arms around me. For the first time ever, Frank Peretti hugged me. Perhaps music played and cherubs fluttered . . . I don't really remember. I was somewhere else—heaven, I think!

We walked, what seemed to be the longest driveway in the world. When we entered the house, he pulled this note from his pocket and read . . .

CHAPTER 2

A Holy Moment

FRANK'S JOURNAL: JUNE 20, 1970

Well, Barb, some people can talk about wild romances. Others about miracles that brought them together, but we more or less sneaked up on each other quietly. I have no amazing story to tell of occurrences that brought us together. All I have is a simple story that materialized out of one, small, quiet, little nothing. This story may never be a bestseller, to some it may even be boring and uneventful.

Christ was of humble birth, so we know that some seemingly humble things do have great importance behind them.

The story is vitally important to me and to you. I guess that's the only appreciation it really needs. I've always wanted things to be simple and uncomplicated. I guess I got what I wanted; a simple, uncomplicated story that you and I can always cherish. We made it short, sweet, and to the point.

In Jesus' name and for His glory, I would like to present the story in its simplest but most beautiful form:

"I love you."

With tear-filled eyes and in a warm embrace, Frank whispered a prayer committing our love and our lives to God.

As a benediction to a beautiful evening, for the first time ever, we tenderly kissed.

A holy moment, a sacred memory.

Frank and I did not have a wild, emotional romance. We agreed it would be that way.

Months before we met, Frank had lost a girlfriend he'd hoped to marry. The warm emotions that had flowed between them quickly cooled because of a few, simple words she penned. Opening the notebook he kept in his shirt pocket, Frank found her message: She loved him and respected him but chose to resign from their relationship.

How does love *resign* from a relationship? She had shattered their dreams. Was her commitment founded in words only?

The romance that once swirled about them quickly hardened like a pond under winter's arctic blast. Frank determined that his emotions would remain sealed in an ice-cold tomb until God brought the girl he was to marry.

CHAPTER 3
Love Never Resigns

Enter . . . me!

Frank's journal records his thoughts:

Barb, I don't know what to think. If you weren't such an imp you'd be downright lovable. Then again, maybe it's your impishness that makes you lovable. I've heard of guys fighting over a girl, but now I find I'm fighting with myself. You and your spiritual zeal! It's enough to make a guy like me love you. Fudge, man, I'm afraid to. Too much of a hassle. So, my soul cries out for you while my logical mind tells my soul to cool it.

Who do I listen to? My logical mind, that's who. Love alone cannot be trusted!

Frank had certainly learned that love alone could not be trusted, so ours became a steady, grow-in-love relationship. Frank often counseled me in the cab of his family's 1942 Dodge Power Wagon. He shared about commitment to God and to love—and the conviction that binds one to those

commitments. We became best friends.

In all fairness to me, when our friendship began taking a turn toward something more serious Frank shared his thoughts honestly with me:

I don't want a girlfriend; I'm looking for a wife. If you want anything less, then we may as well call a halt. I can't be your boyfriend.

Frank didn't want our relationship to grow more serious unless I was ready to consider marriage. But God had already confirmed in my heart His desire for me to marry Frank. If I truly wanted to obey God, my choices had to conform to His will. Vowing to God that I would never resign from my commitment to Frank, I put my convictions on paper:

BARB'S DIARY, SEPTEMBER 1, 1970:

To the one I cherish:

You must know, I will never leave you or dishonor you. I love you and will always remain at your side until our Lord comes to take us home. Our love may be doubted by some, but there are three who know the truth: you, me, and our Lord.

Our love was meant to be. God is the architect of our relationship. I'll always be here to comfort you. I will never betray you. I love you and I respect you, but, unlike another, I will never resign.

"Your God-sent angel"

God brought us together in His will. We were committed to each other and would never resign—that was our conviction. Together, our task will always be to fulfill that promise.

A friend loves at all times. . . .

PROVERBS 17:17

Even during our courtship our roles were defined: Frank was the captain and I was the first mate.

MAY 26, 1970

Hello Frank,

. . . You want a soldier to fight along with you in serving the Lord. I've always seen myself as first mate and my husband as captain of our ship.

MAY 28, 1970

Hello Barb,

. . . You want to be a soldier for God. I told myself what the girl would have to be like. How wonderful to discover that all I wanted was prepackaged in you!

On June 24, 1972, the captain married his first mate.

As a statement of our faith, our wedding cake proclaimed Proverbs 3:6. "In all your ways acknowledge Him, and He will direct your paths."

CHAPTER
4
Sailing Together Through the Seas of Life

Set sail by God, Mr. and Mrs. Frank Peretti embarked upon the Sea of Life.

Frank's job as a studio musician seemed promising. "Studio musicians—earn thirty, sixty dollars an hour." That sounded like great sailing. We had all we needed. Our love for the Lord, our love for each other—and a good paying job!

Foul weather blew in and rocked our little ship.

"They're only paying me $55.00 a week," Frank sighed, sharing about his day sweeping floors and cleaning ashtrays. On top of that, he wasn't getting to play much music.

Whoosh! A wind caught our sails and sent us in a new direction.

The music studio where Frank worked was struggling financially, so in case he found himself without a job, I agreed to work for $1.69 per hour sewing sleeves into letterman's jackets. This was not my idea of married bliss. I cried over our changing circumstances.

Oof! A blast of wind rocked us to our side.

"Welcome to the real world, Mr. and Mrs. Frank Peretti!" The bills signaled that the honeymoon was over: $123.75 for rent, $62.50 car payment for our Volkswagen bus, a few dollars for utilities and Frank's writing course—that left us with $7.50 a week for groceries, which strained my faith a bit, but . . .

Planting our feet firmly on our faith in God, we trusted Him to help us through the storm.

The task I had looked forward to the most became the job I liked the least. Rather than enjoying a weekly trip to the grocery store, I feared the embarrassment that my bill would be more than the money in my purse! My dream of an overflowing pantry kept being washed away by the storm. But God never failed to provide for

In all your ways acknowledge Him, and He shall direct your paths.

PROVERBS 3:6

us, tuna . . . stuffed peppers . . . hot dogs . . . and more tuna!

As we acknowledged God's daily provision, He kept our ship on course.

We were discovering that there is more to sailing through the sea of life than just staying afloat in the water. The blow of each wave reminded us to look beyond the storm and remember that our ship was in God's hands.

Finally, the sea stilled.

It took a strong commitment to each other and a deep trust in God to develop a love that was not easily affected by the difficult circumstances surrounding us. But we made it.

We passed our first sailing test!

And the captain and his first mate are still sailing. Each time the Sea of Life buffets us, we remind ourselves not to lean on our own understanding but to acknowledge our Lord and let Him direct our path.

After six months acclimating to married life, nine months traveling with a music group, and a year living with Frank's folks, we desperately needed some privacy and a place to call our own. Deuteronomy 24:5 says, "When a man has taken a new wife, . . . he shall be free at home one year, and shall cheer up his wife which he has taken."

Believe me, I needed some cheering up!

So we moved into a sweet little cabin set on a hill at the edge of a wood over-looking Puget Sound. Even though it was simply a remodeled chicken coop, it was perfect for our needs— placing parentheses around the next season of our lives. For the next two years we did not feed a career or grow a fertile bank account. Instead, God helped us to establish a love that grew deep and secure under the care of His loving hand.

That remodeled chicken coop sur-rounded by fruit trees became our love

CHAPTER
5
A Season for Love to Blossom

nest. I don't know who was more impas-sioned, the birds cooing under our bed-room eaves, or Frank and I nestled in the warmth of the sun on any given afternoon. We lived at the end of the world and took advantage of the privacy. The perfume of our love, mingled with the sweet smell of wild hyacinth, wafted a fra-grant bouquet to heaven— with which I suspect the Lord was well pleased. As spring flowers bloomed and fruit trees budded, our love for one another unfolded like the white apple blossoms around us.

Inspired by spring, Frank tilled a large plot of ground for a vegetable garden. With a claw-like tool I combed through the dirt, removing weeds and debris. We added fertilizer to the sun-warmed soil, raked it smooth, then planted our seeds, asking God's blessing for an abundant harvest.

By late summer our chins dripped with sweet juice as we savored our first delicious,

As the apple tree among the trees of the wood, so is my beloved among the sons. I sat down under his shadow with great delight, and his fruit was sweet to my taste.

SONG OF SOLOMON 2:3

He who finds a wife finds a good thing, and obtains favor from the LORD.

PROVERBS 18:22

vine-ripened tomatoes. While the kitchen windows steamed up from canning jars of tomatoes, plums, green beans, and cherries, our freezer filled up with apples, carrots, corn, and peas. We stuffed two empty dog-food bags full with freshly dug potatoes. Since our cash was dwindling and there was no immediate prospect of permanent employment, we were especially grateful for the bounty from our garden. God had provided through several long, lean months.

As the seasons come and go, that wonderful hillside garden and our precious season of blossoming love have become sweet, cherished memories—memories of a time when both the garden and our love flourished under attentive care and honest-to-goodness hard work. Through the years, Frank and I have found that the fruit of our love, tended by the careful husbandry of God's hand, is the larder in the pantry that feeds our hearts through the good times and the bad.

"GOD DOESN'T LIE, AND THE BIBLE DOESN'T LIE!" The sermon boomed from the open windows of the country church sitting on the edge of a once-thriving fishing community. Those who built the church had long since passed on, but the little wood-frame building with it's arched windows still offered food for the spiritually hungry and a fold for those in need of the Shepherd. Every Sunday the bell in its steeple rang faithfully, and all who would come were lovingly embraced by the little congregation that Frank and I had so fondly become a part of.

Our sanctuary held about eighty people comfortably. Some mornings, over one hundred glowing faces packed the ancient benches. Centered on the platform was an old, ornate pulpit and behind it a wooden cross hung on plain, painted plasterboard. To the right of the platform sat the proverbial upright piano and to the left, an ancient pipe organ crowned with elaborate, ornamental pipes. An oil stove that belched black smoke, if not properly lit, provided a gathering place to warm our hands. These few items represented the sum total of the embellishments to our simple, country church. Indoor plumbing wouldn't be installed for several more years!

One wouldn't measure the wealth of our little congregation by the offering plate but by the generous service contributed by individuals. Frank led worship on Sunday mornings. A sweet sister prepared communion each month, and we all took our turn at nursery duty. The women organized meals for the sick and needy, and anyone with maintenance skills helped to keep the building and grounds in good repair.

Church attire included granny dresses for the women and bell-bottomed pants for the men. *Both* wore long hair. God was "like really heavy, man," and when someone got saved it was "far out!" Translated that

CHAPTER 6

Little Country Church

meant: we acknowledged God as our sovereign Lord and when someone gave his life to Jesus it was . . . well . . . a miracle!

In today's culture you might describe that little country church as "interactive" and "user friendly." Any feeling of formality quickly dissipated among the open transparency of the people. We were a family, and we benefited from each other's ministry. We didn't have a professional staff to take our burdens to. When a brother or sister needed prayer, the church gathered, laid on hands, and "prayed through" until God gave an answer. We came expecting to do business with God and often, after Bible study, some choruses and hymns, we lingered in prayer and in the presence of God. In those precious moments, tears flowed and hearts softened in the shared rapport of our church family.

This simple, open faith kept Frank and I coming back Sunday after Sunday. When we think back on our experiences there we talk about "the human element" and the "hands-on" type of fellowship and worship that were so precious to us. A more eloquent way to describe it might be "when the mortal touches the eternal and gives it expression through the flesh."

The idea is not new, but it took a little country church on the edge of town to define it for us.

LITTLE COUNTRY CHURCH

Little country church on the edge of town,
People comin' every day from miles around
For meetin's and for Sunday school
And it's very plain to see it's not the way it used to be

Preacher isn't talking' 'bout religion no more
He just wants to praise the Lord
And it's very plain to see it's not the way it used to be

They're talkin' 'bout revival and the need for love
That little church has come alive
Working with each other for the common good
Putting all the past aside

Long hair, short hair, some coats and ties,
People finally comin' around
Lookin' past the hair and straight into the eyes,
People finally comin' around
And it's very plain to see it's not the way it used to be.

Lyrics by CHARLES GIRARD
(USED BY PERMISSION OF EMI MUSIC PUBLISHERS)

In 1976 we left our small-town life so Frank could attend UCLA. In an attempt to regain the sense of community we had left behind, we sought camaraderie among Christian believers. We needed a fellowship of believers who would embrace us into their family.

To our dismay, our experience at one particular church left us feeling just as estranged as the big city life that surrounded us. Our ten months at that church proved quite enlightening. We noticed aloofness hovering about the people prior to services; then almost like theatergoers awaiting the next performance, we were ushered into the sanctuary in a stop-and-go manner similar to our morning commute. When the sanctuary was full, we were directed to an overflow room to watch the service by remote television! And since we never saw the same people twice, we found no more fellowship there than had we stayed at home to watch a service on television.

CHAPTER 7
Big City Church in the Middle of Town

The entire Sunday morning service felt controlled to us and seemed to lack the gentleness of the Spirit that we had experienced back home. We yearned to hear someone ask, "Could you pray with me?" Instead we were instructed to "turn to your neighbor and say _____"—something that came more from a suggestion than from our hearts. We sensed that the schedule and order of the service had become detached engines that pushed the worship to its final chorus and closing prayer. Oh, how our souls longed to linger in the presence of God!

While attending the church, we offered to set up chairs, pass out bulletins . . . anything to feel like we were part of the body. But we became disheartened when our volunteered efforts were never received.

Frank and I called to meet with a pastor, but his impersonal questions left us feeling vaguely like sorted mail, pigeon-

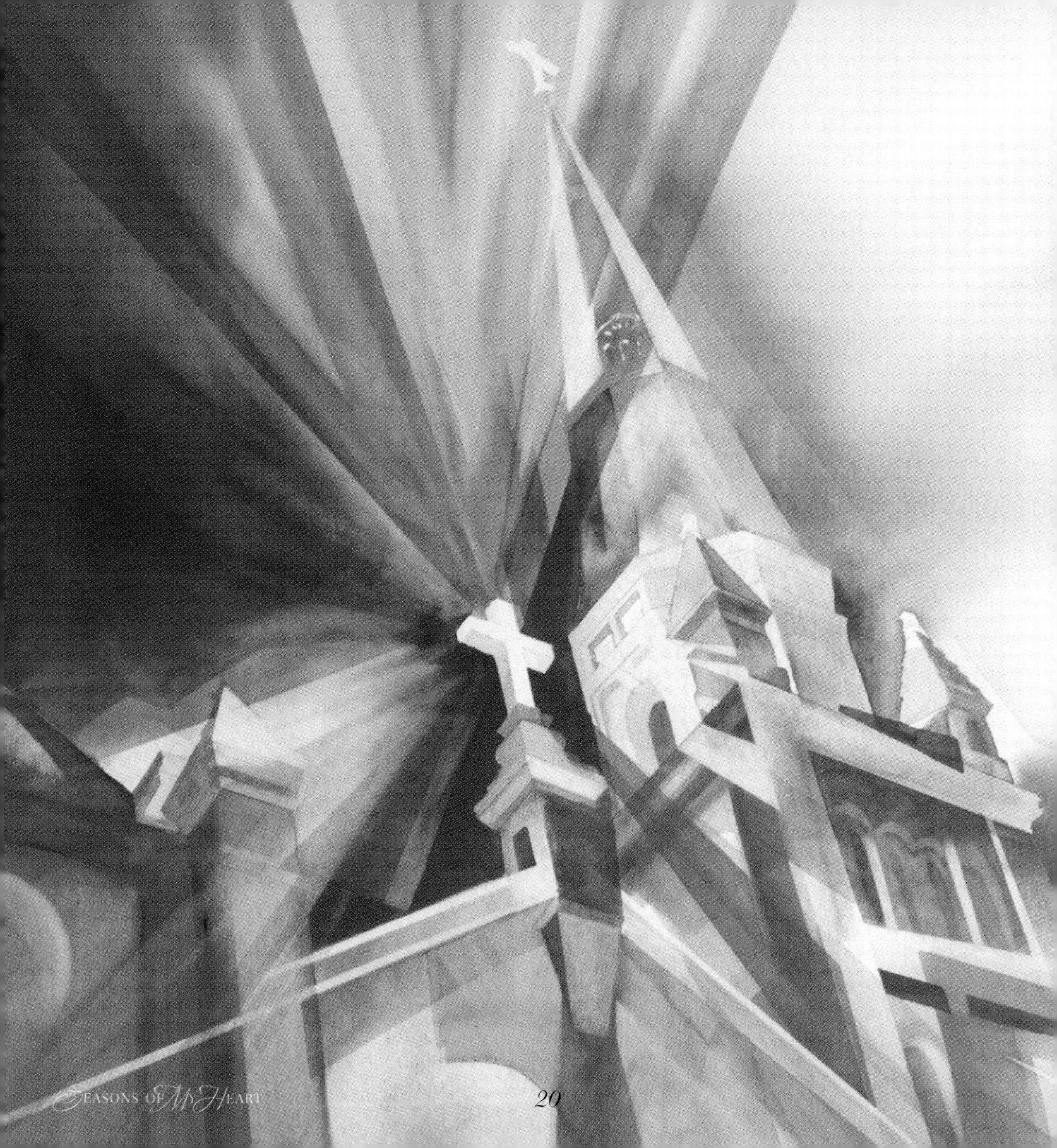

holed into some pastor's counseling specialty. "Are you seeking counsel at this time?" "Do you currently attend Big City Church?" "Is pastor so-and-so teaching a class you attend?"

Within nine months, our Sunday mornings literally ended in tears. Though we were being fed from the pulpit, we were starved for fellowship. We felt like visitors in a foreign country. We couldn't seem to get beyond a simple "Hello." No one ever phoned to say, "Missed seeing you Sunday" or "Just called to see how you're doing."

Then, just at the right time, Frank and I found the intimate fellowship we'd longed for in a church of about seven hundred. Although the congregation was larger than our little country church, the people still welcomed us, prayed with us, and called us by name. Each Sunday God's mercy and grace embraced us. And the mid-week fellowship restored our spirits through new friendships and expressions of love. Once again we enjoyed the intimate worship we had experienced back home.

This church recognized the value of

community and received us into its family in the name of the Lord. The heart of a little country church flowed among the members of this big city church and told us we had come home.

As each one has received a gift, minister it to one another, as good stewards of the manifold grace of God.

1 PETER 4:10

Has God not chosen the poor of this world to be rich in faith and heirs of the kingdom which He promised to those who love Him?

JAMES 2:5

A friend volunteered this advice: When the choices before us all fall within God's will, sometimes He simply asks us which one *we* want to do.

In 1978, while we were still living in Los Angeles, Frank was offered a writing position with one Christian organization and an opportunity to play banjo with another ministry team. At the same time, Frank's father phoned and offered him the position of associate pastor in our little country church back home.

We considered the option of traveling with a ministry team but one thing was certain—Frank didn't want to "drag Barb off on another adventure to who knows where." That left two choices, and I must admit that the opportunity to exchange the concrete and pollution of the city for fresh air and grass under our feet sounded heavenly. The associate pastoral work wouldn't be demanding and would provide time for Frank to write. We con-

cluded that a writer didn't necessarily have to live in Los Angeles to be inspired to write. When the Lord asked, "What do *you* want to do?" the answer from our heart was, *Lord, we just want to go home.*

So we moved into a large, two-story, three-bedroom 1920's parsonage just two blocks from the little country church. The spectacular view from our living room window of the fishing village, Puget Sound, and the Olympic mountains lent inspiration to Frank's writing sessions—which were resulting in some very interesting material.

Down in the village, the single-story mercantile stocked the general grocery and hardware needs of the community—selling everything from Charmin bath tissue to fresh fish on Fridays and extension cords to sink stoppers. Hidden at the back of the building was the town post office. When Flo wasn't wearing her postmaster hat, she manned the cash register and stocked the

CHAPTER
8
What Do You Want to Do?

shelves. Of course when she *was* the postmaster, her cousin Bert managed the store and the two gas pumps out front that dispensed regular and unleaded—when they had fuel.

Every morning around ten o'clock the mercantile was bustling with chatter as people collected groceries, mail, and whatever tidbits of news they could find.

"Mornin' Buster. Saw you haulin' that ole truck outta here yesterday. Bet it took a full week to unbury that thing from under all those blackberries. Good riddance, I say!"

One day Frank moseyed over to the mercantile to see about replacing an outside water faucet. He found a replacement piece in a dilapidated cardboard box sitting on the floor alongside an old box of washers. He blew the dust off looking for a price. *Thirty-nine?*

> *Delight yourself also in the LORD, and He shall give you the desires of your heart.*
>
> PSALM 37:4

"Hey, Flo, the sticker says *thirty-nine.*"

"That's *cents*, and if that's what it says that's what I gotta charge ya. Been meanin' to raise those prices for twenty-years!"

"Noticed you and Barb puttin' in a garden. I've got seed potatoes and onion sets comin' in February, . . . how's your mom? We've been missin' her at bowlin'."

"Sore back," Frank yelled through the slamming screen door as he smiled and thought to himself, *It feels good to be back in this small community where your business is usually not your own and most of the time it doesn't matter anyway!*

Coming home had been the right decision. We had come to a time when our hearts aligned with God's plans and He let us do what *we* wanted to do.

> *A man's heart plans his way, but the LORD directs his steps.*
>
> PROVERBS 16:9

But it didn't always happen that way.

In June of 1980, Frank and I made a down payment on some property and an 8-by-24-foot travel trailer that became our "temporary" home until we could afford to build something permanent.

Two years passed and we were still living scrunched up in our temporary residence—with no money to build. I wrestled with the temptation to take matters into my own hands:

BARB'S DIARY, JANUARY 1, 1982:

I'm wondering if I should find work. I'd like to be able to afford vacations, dinners out, new clothes, and a "real" house. I don't know, though, that the satisfaction of having these "things" could ever outweigh the peace I've found in serving Jesus here at home. I don't know if I could keep an outside job and continue to be all God wants me to be. Sometimes the incentive to get a job is almost unbearable, but the Lord keeps saying, "Trust me and wait."

Frank and I have tried to live our lives pleasing to God, seeking Him in all our decisions. Frank continues to pastor and work on his manuscript when prompted by the Lord. I think God will bless our obedience, and in the joy of serving Him our desires will be realized and Frank will have a writing career.

If we ever have a beautiful home and can live more comfortably, I want to have the assurance that it's not due to something I did but that God allowed it because we were obedient to Him. God says, "If you will, . . . then I will. . . ." If we die to self, then He will fulfill His promises.

The next month I accepted a temporary job to help ease our financial strain yet without being distracted from serving the Lord and helping Frank in his ministry. The first day on the job I was offered a permanent salaried position . . . and turned it down.

CHAPTER
9
Trusting and Waiting

PERETTI RESIDENCE

MASTER PLAN

SCALE
VARIES

PAGE

> *While the picture is in drawing, and the house in building, we see not the beauty of either; but when the artist has put his last hand to them, and given them their finishing strokes, then all appears very good.*
>
> Matthew Henry

Barb's diary, February 4, 1982:

By noon today I was offered a job with an annuity corporation. My response amazed me! Their offer paled beside my desire to do what God has called me to do: to serve at Frank's side. Even though accepting the position would enable Frank and I to build our house, I turned it down. I can't say the offer wasn't tempting, even ego boosting, but I'm learning that obedience to God yields greater, more secure returns.

The job might have provided instant satisfaction of my cravings for the luxury of a "real" house, dinners in restaurants, and a vacation, but in obedience to God I had to die to what I thought we desperately "needed." I was learning that God's plans often take much longer to come to completion than we are willing to endure.

We lived another eight years in that little trailer, obediently yielding our desires to the Lord and learning the value of waiting for His perfect will.

Eventually, the Lord rewarded our patience with a home far above anything we ever dreamed. It did not come to us through anything the world had to offer—it was given to us by God.

We waited . . . and waited . . . and trusted, and in His perfect time God gave us a beautiful home—debt free!

> *My God shall supply all your need according to His riches in glory by Christ Jesus.*
>
> Philippians 4:19

> *The wisdom of this world is foolishness with God.*
>
> 1 Corinthians 3:19

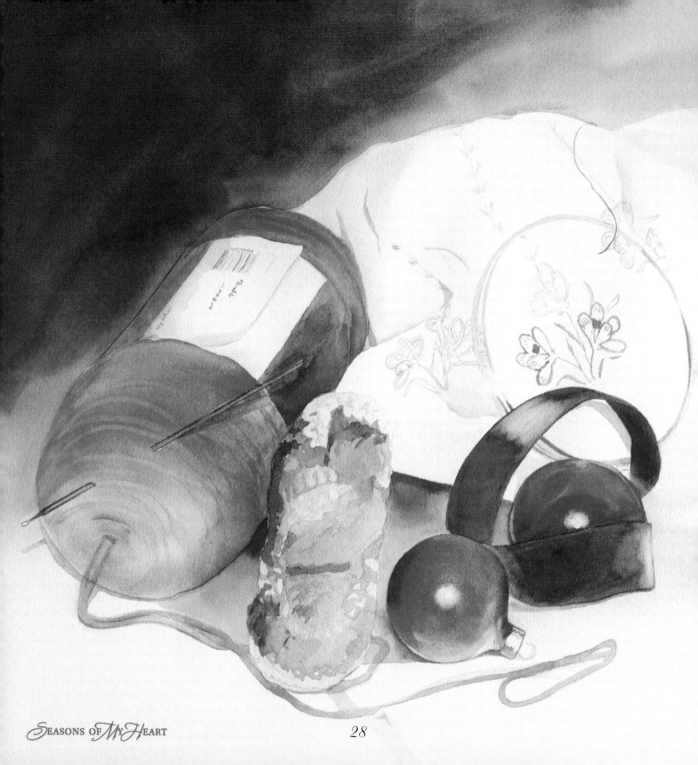

Christmas normally arrives with shopping sprees that produce bundles of gaily wrapped packages tumbling from beneath Christmas trees like swollen rivers. Pantries are filled with delicious delicacies and ribbons, garlands, and lights transform the house.

Our 1982 Christmas appeared to be arriving somewhat more dismally. Frank had found it necessary to supplement our income from the church with construction jobs. But he had not worked in weeks and an expected paycheck for $350 never arrived.

BARB'S DIARY, DECEMBER 14, 1982:

Our finances are extremely low, but our bills are paid and we have food and heat—I actually feel wealthy. Praise God for His provision! With Christmas nearing I should be worried, but I'm at peace.

BARB'S DIARY, JANUARY 9, 1983:

Perhaps because we've been obedient to God and trusted Him for all things, He has

CHAPTER 10

A Most Memorable Christmas

supplied despite our circumstances:

As of December 14 our funds totaled $55.02 for food, heat, bills, Christmas . . . everything!

My girlfriend paid me $10.00 for some booties I had crocheted. I spent $5.00 on food. Then the Lord gave me an idea for Christmas gifts for the family: I could crochet hats for the men and lace collars for the women. Yarn for five hats cost me my other $5.00, my sister-in-law gave me yarn for three more hats, and my mother-in-law supplied enough yarn for another hat. I spent $1.20 on cotton string to finish collars for the women on our list.

With a bankcard we bought my sister and her husband a barbecue as a gift, and the local hardware store let us put another gift on our account. We made our niece and nephew wooden pencil holders in the shape of their names. I found a toy truck and made a wooden matchbox kit for our nephew. I also found a small, embroidered horse I had forgotten about and gave that to our niece along with a crocheted collar. I typed, photocopied, and stapled together shopping lists as gifts for the women.

Dad and Mom gave us $200.00, some of which we used to pay our debt on the bankcard and at the hardware store.

Our trailer insurance came due but because the renewal had not arrived in the mail we didn't have to pay the agency yet!

Friends brought five pounds of hamburger, a steak, cheese, crackers, nuts, and oranges. Another family delivered venison and squash, and dear friends gave Frank a heavy denim jacket and two shirts!

Come to find out, we had withdrawn $10.00 less than what was recorded in our checkbook and our bankcard showed a $15.00 credit.

Frank's motorcycle wasn't running so we cancelled the

All that thrills my soul is Jesus,
He is more than life to me;
And the fairest of ten thousand
In my blessed Lord I see.

THORO HARRIS
"ALL THAT THRILLS MY SOUL"

He satisfies the longing soul, and fills the hungry soul with goodness.

PSALM 107:9

insurance on it, which reduced our bill by $85.00 and added a credit of $20.00 toward our next premium!

Finally, Frank will be speaking for three retreats in January, which will provide additional income.

So our Christmas of 1982 was miraculously transformed from a dismal beginning to a series of joyous celebrations as we witnessed God's sovereignty and abundant provision in our lives. Thoughtful family and friends expressed Jesus' love by stocking our pantry, clothing our backs, and warming our hearts for the season.

Had we not been in such dire need, we would have missed out on the riches we discovered that Christmas. True wealth is not a monetary value but a relationship with Jesus Christ the sovereign God, who knows our needs and cares enough to meet them.

The ringing alarm clock shattered my dream world. As I lay staring at the ceiling, I felt like I had been hit by a truck. I dragged heavy arms and legs from the bed, sorry that we had visited so late the night before. With heavy makeup, I covered the dark rings under my bleary eyes. I grabbed my coffee and spilled it down my blouse, only adding to our crabbiness as Frank and I hurried out the door. Racing desperately to catch the harbor ferry, we had somehow managed to get stuck behind the slowest driver on the island. Irritable thoughts exploded from our heads as we tried to hold our tempers at bay, praying all the while that we would not miss the ferry.

Another late night . . . another early morning . . . three Valentine banquets . . . a weekend youth retreat . . . another seminar . . . and on and on it went. Quiet time with the Lord? Too busy!

CHAPTER 11 Slowing Life Down

BARB'S DIARY, MARCH 8, 1983:

I've been praying, trying to regain an intimacy with the Lord. I'll make a note to avoid our mistake in the future. Here is what has happened:

FEBRUARY

8   *prayer conference*

11, 12, and 14
      Valentine banquets

18–20
      youth retreat

24 and 25
      church growth seminar

25–27
      youth retreat

      meeting with district officials

MARCH

3–5
      church growth seminar and Sunday school seminar

      two morning services, Sunday school, evening service

A man may have but a handful of the world, and yet may enjoy it and himself with a great deal of quietness, with content of mind, peace of conscience, and the love and goodwill of his neighbors.

MATTHEW HENRY

Twenty-eight engagements last month, including regular Sunday and Wednesday services, left us only a few days of rest! We've been so busy with church business we have not had time for the Lord!

I've learned that if we don't rest, find time to meditate, pray, and read the Bible, then we become incompetent to do the Lord's work. By the time Frank and I had a day off, I was depressed and had lost any sense of the serenity I had gained in quiet meditation with the Lord.

Looking back on our life then, I am reminded of the river that races by our house during spring runoff. Dirtied and muddied by debris from its harried race, it overflows its banks, galloping at tremendous speeds along its course like a racehorse out of control. Frank and I had become as out of control as that river, darting from engagement to engagement,

cluttering our spiritual walk with just too many things. We had no time to think, no time for leisure. We were simply rushing to the next bend, on to the next destination.

Then God showed us a better way.

When spring turns to summer the river current slows down and flows past our home at a much more leisurely pace. It seems unhurried to arrive at its destination, almost as though meditating on the creation of God that is reflected in its mirror-like surface.

We've learned a lesson from the calm summer river—*slow down*! The dirt and debris that muddied our spiritual walk disappeared downstream as we uncluttered our lifestyle. We rest now by the river's edge, in awe of God's beauty that surrounds us. As we've slowed to the pace of our leisurely river, these two less-frenzied souls now seek to reflect God's beauty as He ministers His gentle peace.

Better a handful with quietness then both hands full, together with toil and grasping for the wind.

ECCLESIASTES 4:6

33

It was secondhand plywood that had been used to ship pipes, but at a dollar a sheet we could afford it. We could saw it into twelve-inch strips, and it would suffice for lapped siding on the little "shack" we were building.

We had been living in our 24-foot trailer for three years when Frank's folks offered to purchase the building materials for an addition. My folks bought the insulation, and Frank and I found seven windows at a bargain price of $135.00. Friends gave us three doors.

We were expanding our living space from 192 square feet to a spacious 648 square feet! It would be wonderful! We would be able to pass each other without bumping. We would have room for a washer and a refrigerator, and instead of sleeping on the folded dinette, we could have a real bed! We were graduating to a whole new way of life!

CHAPTER
12
There's
No Place
Like Home

But as a dreary winter dampened Puget Sound, it also dampened our rosy enthusiasm. The twelve-degree weather was unusual for our area as was stuffing blankets into cracks to ward off thirty-five-mile-per-hour winds. Our snug summer cottage had turned into a drafty shack! Our only source of heat was a wood stove, which made life at least tolerable . . . for a while.

What was that peculiar odor? Was it dirt? A gas leak? No. A rat had escaped the bitter cold by crawling into our cabin, only to die in the warmth of our insulation! We couldn't afford to put sheet rock on the walls so the insulation was bare to the room. Peeling away the brown-papered fluffy stuff in search of the carcass, Frank finally found the long, slender tail dangling between two insulation bats.

This couldn't continue. We felt like hardened criminals listening to the traps snap in the night.

Then there was the environmentally correct composting toilet housed in its own little shack just a short stroll from our door. Frank's job was to keep the aerobic composting alive by stirring it once a week—a job he never looked forward to!

Again I wondered if we would ever have a real house with a toilet that flushed. Could life be any worse? Yes . . . and for many it is.

I certainly didn't appreciate even the little home I had until I spent some time away from it. While traveling with Frank to numerous speaking engagements, I actually began to long for our little "shack." The Lord spoke to my heart that I had grown unappreciative of His provision. Although it wasn't very much, it was our home. Perhaps it would be our *only* home.

With a change in attitude I decided that even if our home was only a little shack, it was going to be the cutest, cleanest shack on the block. With bucket in

I have learned in whatever state I am, to be content: I know how to be abased, and I know how to abound.

PHILIPPIANS 4:11

hand I washed and bleached the plywood floors. A carefully placed mirror and bookshelves helped hide the trailer siding that formed one "wall" of the living room. We couldn't afford fancy decorations and knick-knacks, so I twisted grapevines from our yard into wreaths and adorned them with dried flowers and empty eggshells. They looked adorable hanging from the rafters. A cute tin can that sheltered a bouquet of wild flowers added a spot of cheery color to the drab room.

It wasn't glitzy or glamorous, but it was warm and livable, it was our home, and I thanked God for the shelter it provided.

And having food and clothing, with these we shall be content.

1 TIMOTHY 6:8

Frank's salary from the church didn't quite pay the bills, so honorariums from other speaking engagements in the Seattle area kept us from falling into debt. While the demand for Frank's speaking increased through the years, the times between engagements were opportunities for my faith in God's provision to increase.

Many times the logic of our natural circumstances cried out, *You're not going to make it if you trust only in God to provide for you.* But a stronger voice in our hearts kept encouraging us, *Hold on tight to Jesus' hand and time will prove that He can be trusted.*

BARB'S DIARY, FEBRUARY 17, 1983:

As of today there is nothing scheduled for outside ministry in March and April except for Spiritual Emphasis Week at the Christian school.

CHAPTER 13
Trusting Jesus to Lead the Way

We're living pretty much hand-to-mouth, paying our bills as the money comes in.

I don't know what the Lord has in mind, but I'm peacefully confident He is in control. Thank you Lord! Maybe Frank will get more speaking engagements, but if not he will have more time to work on his manuscript.

BARB'S DIARY, FEBRUARY 18, 1983:

I've been praying that Frank would become the man God wants him to be. It seems the Lord has whispered Proverbs 31:23 into my heart, "Her husband is known in the gates, when he sits among the elders of the land."

Today we received a letter from our district camp director. The letter began "Dear Reverend Peretti." The director said he wasn't sure if Frank was a reverend, but after Frank's stint as camp speaker the camp committee revered him indeed.

Presumption boasts, "If the sea be before you, march into it and expect a miracle." But Faith listens neither to Presumption nor to Despair, nor to Cowardice . . . but it hears God say, "Stand still" and immovable as a rock it stands.

CHARLES H. SPURGEON
MORNING AND EVENING

What an honor to be distinguished in that way! I pondered these things as the Lord reassured me that His hand was upon us.

BARB'S DIARY, FEBRUARY 22, 1983:

I'm beginning to feel that God is doing a new work in Frank's ministry. At times I feel I could be married to a famous man someday. What would it be like if God placed us in that position? . . . "Lord, if this is your will, prepare our hearts."

My scheduled Bible reading took me to Proverbs twenty-two. Verses one and two say, "A good name is to be chosen rather than great riches, loving favor rather than silver and gold. The rich and the poor have this in common, the LORD is the maker of them all."

Verse twenty-nine says, "Do you see a man who excels in his work? He will stand before kings; he will not stand before unknown men."

Many years have passed since I read those verses. I had no idea Frank's writing and speaking would lead us to where we are now. I didn't know where Jesus was leading, but I sensed His hand taking ours—and we were willing to follow.

Whether we have millions of dollars in the bank or live hand-to-mouth, true riches come from living a life that is pleasing to the Lord. As Frank and I daily slip our hands into the hand of Jesus, we strive to honor Him in all we do, and He continues to lead us along paths we could never have imagined.

Life is much smoother when we trust Jesus to lead the way.

Be of good courage, and He shall strengthen your heart, all you who hope in the LORD.

PSALM 31:24

I remember standing on an old cedar stump overlooking the property that was adjacent to our own. Maple trees spread their leafy canopy over the deep ravine and lush undergrowth, while vying with towering cedars and hemlock for sunlight. Our dream was that the abundant blackberries, foxgloves, and salal growing in the shaded woodland soil would one day be ours, providing the privacy Frank and I desperately longed for. Frank took my hand and prayed, "Lord, if it be your will, we would like to buy this property someday."

BARB'S DIARY, FEBRUARY 16, 1983:

Though we have no money, today we asked the Lord if we could purchase the lots next to us. I trust if this is God's plan, He will provide. Our responsibility now is to wait until God makes it available.

Deuteronomy 11:8 says, "Therefore you shall keep every commandment which I command you today, that you may be strong, and go in and possess the land which you cross over to possess. . . ."

CHAPTER 14
Canaan **II**

God gave that original promise in Deuteronomy to the Israelites as they left the bondage of Egypt and entered Canaan, the Promised Land. Even before we were married, God gave Frank and I this same promise: If we would be faithful to do all He asked of us, our every need would be provided.

We called the property next door Canaan II because we hoped that through patience and obedience God would one day allow us to buy our own Promised Land. It was not fantasy or wishful thinking. God had proven time and again that He could provide when we waited on Him. His blessings had always come with no sorrow attached.

I reflected on how God always kept His promises when we were willing to be obedient and wait on Him.

BARB'S DIARY, FEBRUARY 16, 1983:

In 1980 the Lord provided a down payment for property we wanted to buy from a landowner who wasn't interested in selling. Through God's intervention, we now live on that property in a trailer miraculously furnished to us because we refused to disobey God's commands.

After reviewing our financial situation and finding that Frank and I had no credit history, the trailer salesman required a cosigner on our loan. Because we believe the Bible teaches against cosigning, we told the salesman we would not be buying the trailer.

> *Most assuredly,*
> *I say to you,*
> *whatever you ask*
> *the Father in*
> *My name He will*
> *give you.*
> JOHN 16:23

Then we asked God if He would somehow lift the cosigner requirement.

The next morning the salesman called. Through renegotiations the requirement was no longer needed. God had provided!

Through no direct planning on our part, exactly five years from the day we had asked God for Canaan II, I recorded this in my diary:

BARB'S DIARY, FEBRUARY 16, 1988:

We signed the closing papers today on

> *These . . . are the evidences of true biblical faith:*
> *(1) you are willing to wait (2) you are concerned*
> *only for the glory of God (3) you are obeying God's*
> *Word (4) you have God's joy and peace within*
> WARREN W. WIERSBE
> BE OBEDIENT

Canaan II. God provided $10,000.00 down on a ten-year contract. Even our budget is not affected. Our new payment replaces what we were paying on our old contract!

When we allow God to have sovereign control in our lives we free Him to work for our highest good. Through God's provision our property was paid in full by 1989. We were debt free! God had abundantly provided . . . again!

How can I thank a God who so generously cares for me? I can thank Him through a heart that patiently waits and obediently follows His instructions.

Whatever wilderness Frank and I have faced—whether praying for food on our table or for the finances to pay our bills, whether for help in purchasing a property or in writing a book—when we have patiently waited, God has always led us to our Canaan Land.

Frank was invited to be the speaker for a youth retreat in southwest Washington. Upon our arrival we found ourselves nestled deep in the foothills of the towering but now silent volcano, Mt. Saint Helens. Monumental rock formations rising majestically over a sparkling stream provided a breathtaking backdrop for the weekend. Warm dappled sunlight sparkled through a dense forest of evergreen trees that provided a haven for the birds. Inspiration filled my soul, and what began as a simple solitary hike along a footpath into the Cispus National Forest transformed into an endearing memory.

BARB'S DIARY, FEBRUARY 19, 1983:

Light was shining through the trees, bouncing off tiny water droplets that clung to branches in the moist air. Over the trail, which was intercepted now and then by a small, mountain brook, hovered patches of low mist slowly dissipating in the afternoon sun. A breeze rippled through the leaves

CHAPTER 15

Alone with the Father

above, plundering the early budding bushes with showers of dewdrops and fanning my face with its first hint of spring. "Um-m-m," I thought, "such peace and tranquility."

The beauty of the forest so moved me I was drawn into worship. A song emerged from my innermost being:

"Come away, my beloved, partake with Me."

Before I could utter another sound it seemed as though the words were carried heavenward on a current of air, freeing them from their earthly bounds, becoming an offering of praise to the Creator of this sanctuary.

More lyrics so thoroughly intermingled with the joy and anticipation abounding within me, that I couldn't be sure if the worship originated from within me or simply came from heaven above:

"The beauty of the Lord is calling me. Come away with Me, My beloved, come away."

Field and forest,
vale and mountain,
Flowery meadow,
flashing sea,
Chanting bird and
flowing fountain,
Call us to rejoice in
Thee.

Henry Van Dyke

Deeper into the forest I followed, awestruck by the three-hundred-and-sixty-degree masterpiece enfolding me. I knew the artist personally! Such beauty, yet only a dim reflection of my Savior's wondrous majesty! He created me also and for this afternoon we were alone. His peace and serenity held me.

With His Spirit embracing mine, as though carried on the wings of a bird, we left the heavy humid air of the lower elevation and soared to the crisp, fresh air above. At the top of the trail God's creation filled me with its own serenade. A steady cadence carried by the tumbling brook was accentuated with syncopated rhythms crooned by the tree frogs. Birds lilted their melodies while the leaves rustled their descant—a veritable symphony of surround sound! Truly God's glorious beauty had won my heart.

The Spirit wooed, "Come away my dear one, rest in My presence."

My heart warmly conceded, "I will follow You, Lord. Forever I will be yours."

The sovereign, awesome Creator ordained this very moment and desired this afternoon with me. Goose bumps encompassed me. Tears filled my eyes.

Miraculous visions of glory would be hard-pressed to supersede the splendor of those few cherished hours. Enveloping me with monumental, unconditional love, God Almighty authenticated intimate fellowship in that holy, forested sanctuary and touched a sympathetic passion deep within my soul.

I have not sought to fully understand what transpired that day, but in the Father's wisdom He created that sympathetic passion within me that, when touched by the finger of God, engaged intimate fellowship, causing me once again to concede:

"Take me away Lord, I will follow You. Forever I will be yours."

The fig tree puts forth her green figs,
And the vine with the tender grapes
give a good smell.
Rise up, my love, my fair one,
And come away!

Song of Solomon 2:13

BARB'S DIARY, MARCH 31, 1984:

I've never seen Frank or myself so stressed . . . almost to tears! We believe the Lord is pushing us in a new direction.

We've had enough Easter plays, Christmas plays, choir practices, Sunday school preparation, worship leading, youth meetings, retreats, conferences, board meetings, and outside speaking engagements to make us ill!

Frank's fairly certain he'll be taking a leave of absence from the pastorate in May. He can do carpentry work and maybe get some writing done. That's still his number one desire. We need this month to seek the Lord's direction. We're really in the dark about what to do.

Frank had been an associate pastor for nearly five years in our little country church. Gradually we began to feel wearied of preparing for Sunday night services only to have two people come. The burden of feeling responsible for the people in our congregation and trying to decide what new things we could do with all the kids caused us to wonder if perhaps we did not have a pastor's heart.

But rather than step down from our responsibilities we remained in the pastorate, placing our trust in the security and salary of that position rather than in God. That mistake triggered a long and painful burnout season that lasted several years. God in His mercy slowly removed His anointing and forced us to re-evaluate our motives.

Frank and I talked at lunch today. He has been sensing the same thing I have: the ministry is fading. It feels like a season coming to an end.

Being in the ministry had forced us to grow, and we had produced fruit for God's kingdom through our teaching and counseling efforts. But now we felt exhausted and wondered what in the world we were

CHAPTER
16
God
Puts His
Plow to
Our Lives

doing in the pastorate. The level of stress and tension came to such a point that if Frank had been asked to lead one more worship service or if I had been asked to lead one more woman's meeting we both would have "lost it."

Each passing day found us more removed from our church work. Our patience and nerves were worn to a frazzle. We felt completely spent. Much like an autumn garden, we had come to the end of a fruitful season.

We needed a rest. We felt as though we had nothing left to give.

It was time to let God cultivate the depleted residue of our lives. Little did we realize that with each painful pass of the plow, He was actually preparing us for new growth and a most unique ministry.

Strength and encouragement came through a word from Frank's older brother:

APRIL 18, 1984

"Like Abraham, be patient. God's plans for you are greater than you could imagine.

Indeed I am for you, and I will turn to you, and you shall be tilled and sown.

EZEKIEL 36:9

In His perfect will we can accomplish more in one day than if we struggle seventy years under our own power."

His message fell like gentle showers on the tilled furrows of our hearts, watering our withered hopes.

God allowed our worn-out lives to lay dormant a season. And gradually, where pain once lay buried, a deeply rooted faith began to grow. As we let our lives be tilled by God's holy plow, we learned patience and trust.

We learned that it takes time and tilling for God's abundance to be reaped in our lives.

Our Lord in His infinite wisdom and superabundant love, sets so high a value upon His people's faith that He will not screen them from those trials by which faith is strengthened. While the wheat sleeps comfortably in the husk it is useless to men. It must be threshed out of its resting place before its value can be known.

CHARLES H. SPURGEON
MORNING AND EVENING

It was over, a season ended. We left the pastorate feeling worthless, destitute, . . . miserable.

Frank, walking stooped from the mounting burdens he carried, muttered painfully, "I've failed as a musician, failed to finish college, failed in the pastorate, and now I'm failing as a provider!"

BARB'S DIARY, MAY 3, 1984:

Yesterday Frank and I talked about our future and his career. I'm feeling like a car at 200,000 miles expected to go another 100,000. I don't know if I can. Frank will have to doctor me, but he's not doing well himself.

He feels he must write but isn't sure how he'll support us. That overwhelms me! Neither of us has the strength to face such uncertainty. Tears fell from our eyes as Frank asked the Lord to strengthen us.

Our prayers seemed like a one-ended conversation. Had someone asked, "What are you hearing from God?" we might have growled, "Nothing!"

One *possible* hope lay in a novel, now four inches thick, to which Frank had dedicated five years of his spare time. Concerned friends and family hinted that a college degree would have offered more hope but *The Heavenlies* was the main force driving Frank. It didn't offer much hope, but it was the *only* hope we had.

BARB'S DIARY, MAY 14, 1984:

It hurts when people ask, "Will Frank go back to school?" As though a college education was the sure cure for our woes! All I can reply is Frank needs to write. Acting outside God's guidance, his efforts are vain. God does not require things on which we depend to execute His plans. He only requires our obedience.

It seemed in those day that our obedience was rewarded by a rather destitute lifestyle with no great revelations offered

CHAPTER 17

Establish the Work of Our Hands

> *When we consider that God is infinitely wise, righteous, faithful, and that He is a God of judgment, we shall see no reason to despair of belief in Him, but all the reason in the world to hope in Him, that it will come in due time, in the best time.*
>
> MATTHEW HENRY

from a silent God. Life definitely did not get better.

Frank has done some carpentry work, but we have no foreseeable source of steady income and no speaking engagements scheduled for a few months. He's applied for a woodworking job.

At least Frank's unique gift for writing and speaking drew encouraging comments from those who heard him speak and read his manuscript. "Your manuscript blessed my socks off, but I'm not able to use it. " "Great message! You ought to write a book!" Such distinguished recognition raised our spirits but never led anywhere except to disappointment and frustration. Maybe someday . . .

Perhaps stepping down from the pastorate is just another turn in our road and by waiting on the Lord we'll find a new ministry around that corner.

We kept calling out to God; we needed Him fiercely. Occasionally we thought we heard a faint small voice directing, *"Frank, just write the book"* . . . but then silence.

One morning with *The Heavenlies* lying before us Frank took my hand and prayed Psalm 90:17:

" . . . let the beauty of the Lord our God be upon us: and establish the work of our hands . . ."

"Just write the book" was all we knew to do. This was the directive Frank followed. But before us lay a long, silent season— one that God used to build His character in our lives.

It was years before we could truly declare *"The Lord has established the work of our hands."*

> *A man's heart plans his way, but the LORD directs his steps.*
>
> PROVERBS 16:9

BARB'S DIARY, SUMMER 1984:

"Hope deferred makes the heart sick: but when the desire comes, it is a tree of life." Proverbs 13:12

I am experiencing Proverbs 13:12. Hope deferred for so long has made my heart sick. My stomach is in knots. I feel weak, drained. I haven't felt happy in a long while. Frank prayed for me last night and this morning.

Our emotions daily teetered on the edge of total spiritual and emotional burnout. The slightest push in the wrong direction would surely have sent Frank and I tumbling into an ever-growing chasm of distance between us and the church. Five years in the ministry had left us spiritually exhausted and financially bankrupt. Our living situation had not progressed beyond the travel trailer with a shack around it and a composting toilet outside our back door. Mice remained our nightly visitors.

We despaired in not knowing God's plans for us. Doubts haunted us. *"God said He came that you might have abundant life."* Well, we had not seen it! *"Shall you accept good from God and not trouble?"*

We had both been brought up to believe that God alone was the One on whom we could depend. Yet favorite Christian phrases like "Give it all to Jesus," "God will care for you," and "Lay it on the altar," were now placebos that lacked effectiveness. They stung like salt poured on the wounds of our hearts. Surprisingly to us, the church seemed to provide only increasing spiritual activities, not answers to our dilemma. Our only hope for peace of mind and our only assurance came from God's Word. We depended on it . . . we clung to it.

BARB'S DIARY, SEPTEMBER 1, 1984:

We've been asking the Lord not to tempt us beyond what we can endure. Many times I have thought about our faithful tithing and giving, challenging God with His own words, "Where is your promise, of pouring out a

CHAPTER 18

Hope Deferred

There is a lighthouse out at sea: it is a calm night—I cannot tell whether the edifice is firm. The tempest must rage about it, and then I shall know whether it will stand. So with the Spirit's work: if it were not on many occasions surrounded with tempestuous waters, we should not know that it was true and strong. . . .

CHARLES SPURGEON
MORNING AND EVENING

We agree, however, that if we can't trust God, we have nowhere to turn. No one else has the answers.

For everything there is a season . . . My married years have been a continuous season of waiting, hoping. Who knows why? If we'll obey and wait, God will keep His promises and so, though He be silent, I continue waiting.

Waiting . . . hoping . . . we lived each day literally moment by moment, waiting for some door to open. Perhaps a phone call, something in the mail . . .

blessing we can't contain? We can barely make ends meet!" We could use good news to put fat on our bones because hope deferred these twelve married years has made our hearts sick.

I remember lying in bed, sighing deeply, fighting the temptation to give in to the pressure of doubt and despair that weighed heavily upon us. These unsettling adversaries were testing us daily. *"You've failed, God doesn't care for you!"*

Day by day we had to remind ourselves that God *did* care. Only by trusting Him could we learn to accept difficult times and not just good times. And eventually, He did fulfill more than our deepest desires, but the ensuing months brought no phone calls . . . no letters with good news to fatten our bones. Silence and hardship continued, deferring our hope and making our hearts sick—but not dead.

We were down but not ready to give up.

God did care, and we needed to give Him the opportunity to prove it.

The ransomed of the LORD shall return, and come to Zion with singing, with everlasting joy on their heads. They shall obtain joy and gladness, and sorrow and sighing shall flee away.

ISAIAH 35:10

I'm expected to go to a women's meeting. . . . I shudder at the thought! The church consumes our time, but these days I'm finding closer communion with God at home!

Frank and I should have dropped everything when we left the pastorate. It's not that we're deserting the Lord, for in turning from Him we lose valuable riches! Our lives are fulfilled only in Him.

I had been deceived by the illusion that holiness was measured in hours spent giving oneself to the *church.* Continually bending to this coercion seemed to appease the delusion for a while, but eventually, instead of feeling the joy of Christian fellowship when I went to church, I wept in my pew. Like an autumn tree casually disrobed of its leaves, it seemed that the years of time-consuming ministry in the church had finally stolen away the sweet presence of Jesus that had once awaited me there.

Last Sunday I had another emotional morning. I had planned to go to church but grew hesitant and resistant. Finally, I just could not go. Entering the living room I saw Frank's guitar and Bible sitting by the door; I wanted to scream! I didn't understand my feelings; I didn't want to have them.

I pleaded with Frank to stay; I needed him. With his arms enfolding me, we decided a long time had passed since attending church had been a pleasurable thing we did together. Our problem was we'd become enslaved to the church, which had forced itself between us and our relationship to the Lord. Our ministry in the church was always calling us away from home and each other. It hurt!

Few understood what Frank and I were experiencing—ministerial burnout. Unnerving as it was, we felt repulsed by anything to do with church. Our years of giving out and giving out had left us not

CHAPTER
19
Beside Still Waters

Delight in divine service is a token of acceptance. Those who serve God with a sad countenance, because they do what is unpleasant to them, are not serving Him at all. They bring the form of homage, but the life is absent. Our God requires no slaves to grace His throne; He is the Lord of the empire of love, and would have His servants dressed in the livery of joy.

CHARLES H. SPURGEON
MORNING AND EVENING

only physically and emotionally fatigued but spiritually drained as well.

With a caring shepherd's wisdom our new pastor identified our hurts and helped us to see that our souls desperately needed to be refreshed. As the prescribed medicine to heal our wounds, he relieved us of all responsibility to the church and participation in ministry. It felt unnatural to stay home Sunday mornings, but we knew we needed to have some time away from the church before we would ever feel like being a part of it again.

Our pastor counseled us to spend time in God's Word, allowing it to restore our souls. We took our medicine faithfully,

spending much time meditating on the Psalms and the Proverbs. Psalm 23 especially ministered to us again and again:

He makes me to lie down in green pastures; He leads me beside the still waters. He restores my soul . . .

The "green pastures" provided by the Lord flanked a three-mile loop that Frank and I loved to walk. Strolling hand in hand, the road before us seemed to transform into our still waters; it brought rest to our souls. There and in other quiet moments we experienced a refreshingly new kind of worship and close, nurturing friendship with Jesus that we had never known before.

As we walked through this "valley of death," the medicine prescribed by our wise shepherd became a healing salve in the hand of the Great Shepherd, who gently loved us and cared for us while leading us beside our still waters.

The LORD is my shepherd; I shall not want. He makes me to lie down in green pastures; He leads me beside the still waters.

PSALM 23:1–2

BARB'S DIARY, OCTOBER 19, 1984:

One of the benefits to all this testing we've been going through is that we have nothing left to place our trust in but God. I feel now that we're beginning to truly live in God's kingdom. Any hope we may have had in this world now rests in Christ alone; Jesus is all we have.

When Frank and I married in 1972 we set sail on the Sea of Life. By 1984 quite a storm had begun to swell that deluged us with wave after wave of discouragement and despair. We were persistently engulfed with poverty. We had no assurance that our bills would be paid or that there would be food on our table. The telephone never rang with promises of writing contracts and there was nothing in the mailbox that would secure our future. Instead, we nearly drowned in discouragement. Depression pounded against our faith and trust in God's promises then ebbed away, leaving us draped in failure like seaweed splayed across the sand.

BARB'S DIARY, DECEMBER 28, 1984:

After completing a youth retreat tomorrow Frank plans to apply at the ski factory or contact his old employers for some kind of work.

We have less than $50.00 in checking and $450.00 in savings. That's the sum total of our net worth. I will be looking for a part-time job in January.

We've submitted Frank's manuscripts but without some type of previously published work that might open the door, prayer and a miracle are the only keys we now hold that might possibly unlock an opportunity in the publishing industry. So, that's what we're dependent on: God, prayer, and a miracle. In that order!

News that a publisher was at least interested in Frank's writing brought a ray of sunshine to a year that had proved to be

CHAPTER
20

Tempest Tossed

*In seasons of severe trial, the Christian
has nothing on earth that he can trust to,
and is therefore compelled to cast himself
on his God alone. When his vessel is on
its beam-ends, and no human deliverance
can avail, he must simply and entirely
trust himself to the providence and care
of God. Happy storm that wrecks a man
on such a rock as this!*

CHARLES H. SPURGEON,
MORNING AND EVENING

one of our most turbulent. To say this news brought encouragement would be an understatement! Maybe God *was* planning to perform a miracle!

We were living in a completely undulating state. Our spirits would swell with the hope of good news one day and then plunge to despair the next. Frank felt strongly that he was called to be a writer, and many people had spoken positively about his talent, yet others reminded us of the discouraging truth of the situation, "Do you know there are hundreds of manuscripts that cross an editor's desk each month?" "Only a few fortunate people can actually make a living as a writer."

Even the smallest bit of good news was a ray of sunshine, bringing hope that there would one day be an end to our cloudy days, but it was still too early to say the storm had ended. The ebb and flow of the waves around us kept us continually on the edge of tension. Each day we had to decide, *Will we let our situation drive us to discouragement or will we trust God's leading and remain faithful to Him?*

Time after time, day by day, God helped us to remain faithful to Him and to His calling for our lives.

There are still storms that come, and the wind and waves still assail our ship, but we have found that if we hold tight onto Jesus the Solid Rock, He is steadfast and immovable. He always keeps us safe in His hand.

*Those who go down to the sea in ships,
Who do business on great waters,
They see the works of the LORD,
And His wonders in the deep.*

PSALM 107:23–24

"A violent earthquake shook the cave. Jay sought for any glimpse of his father through the dust. Rubble cluttered the passageways. He shined his flashlight, frantically searching. Finally, he located his father lying face down . . .

ANOTHER QUAKE! A huge rock loosened above his father's body, 'DAD'!! But it was too late, the boulder was falling . . ."

That's how Frank ended the second morning of chapel at the 1983 Cedar Springs junior-high summer camp. Frank's plan was to bait the kids with tantalizing stories so they would be excited for next morning's chapel. It was a huge success! Dying to hear more of the story, the kids offered Frank bribe after bribe to hear the rest of the story, but he wouldn't budge. He dramatized one installment at a time giving each it's own unique cliffhanger ending. At week's end both the counselors and kids were applauding, and the general consensus was "You should have that published!"

So after camp, when he wasn't pounding nails, Frank pounded out a proposal on his electric Royal Medallion II typewriter. We still lived in the trailer with finances at poverty level, but now we had new hope: An entire camp of kids had testified that Frank could, indeed, write a story that would keep them turning pages. What did we have to lose?

Nearly a year and a half after Frank wrote the original story we received promising news:

CHAPTER 21
We Heard the Birds Singing

BARB'S DIARY, OCTOBER 15, 1984:

October 1st we heard from Crossway Books. They're interested in <u>The Door In the Dragon's Throat</u> and will discuss it at their next executive meeting.

We are extremely excited, and have been praying specifically that: by the end of the year we would find a publisher for <u>The</u>

The people who walked in darkness have seen a great light; those who dwelt in the land of the shadow of death, upon them a light has shined.

ISAIAH 9:2

BARB'S DIARY, NOVEMBER 6, 1984:

Frank and I sent the completed manuscript of <u>The Door In the Dragon's Throat</u> to Crossway Books. We are really praying for its publication! Frank, Mom, and I are typing the final chapter of <u>The Heavenlies</u> as Crossway has decided to review it as well.

BARB'S DIARY, JANUARY 11, 1985:

Crossway has decided to publish <u>The Door In The Dragon's Throat</u>, and they may be interested in publishing more kid's books!

Praise the Lord!

<u>The Heavenlies</u> has received favorable reviews and will be considered for publication at Crossway's next meeting. We celebrated <u>Heavenlies</u> and that <u>The Door In the Dragon's Throat</u> would be published with requests for more kid's books.

on Saturday using a ten-dollar gift certificate for dinner. It was the eve of Frank's 34th birthday so we commemorated both special occasions.

We can hardly believe this is happening! We'll continue to pray for the publication of <u>The Heavenlies</u>. "Good news puts fat on the bones!"

It was like seeing light at the end of the tunnel or the beginning of a new season. A quote one friend shared with us seemed so appropriate,

"Faith is the bird that senses the light and sings while dawn is still dark."

We had lived with dreariness and disappointment for so very long. Though this one little book would not pay all the bills, and uncertainty still surrounded us, we sensed the light peeking through our darkness. After a long season of silence we heard the birds singing and knew deep in our hearts that our dawn would eventually come.

In the shadow of His hand He has hidden Me, and made Me a polished shaft; in His quiver He has hidden Me.

ISAIAH 49:2

FLASH!!! Lightening. FLASH!! Again. Then again! Our bedroom erupts in a strobe light display. CRRRAACK! Thunder rumbles the house and ear-shattering hail pelts our metal roof. Yet the security and warmth of our mountain home reminds me of God's protection when one of life's "summer storms" pelted our faith.

BARB'S DIARY, JANUARY 17, 1985:

We have $24.00 in savings, $4.50 in checking, and $80.00 left from my folk's Christmas gift. I was out of laundry and dish soap so I withdrew $20.00 to buy soap and gas.

We're taking each day as it comes. I'm trusting God's faithfulness! I'm applying for work and Frank applied again at the ski factory. In the meantime he's working on "Tilly," an audio drama.

BARB'S DIARY, JANUARY 28, 1985:

Frank was hired! It'll be a few weeks before he begins the newly created part-time position they have offered him. We need the money now, but God knows our future, and I am learning that He provides for our every need. Anyway, this job will allow Frank time to pursue speaking and writing. The Lord is taking care of us; one day at a time the bills are paid.

Our food supply is low, but I still have Christmas money I could spend. Frank earned $135.00 speaking for a retreat. That will be used to pay the power bill and our tithe, and to buy chicken feed.

Psalm 66:8–11 says, "Oh bless our God, you peoples! And make the voice of His praise to be heard, who keeps our soul among the living, and does not allow our feet to be moved. For You, O God, have tested us; You have refined us as silver is refined. You have brought us into the net; you laid affliction on our backs."

I recognize the trial, but this time I feel sheltered in His care.

CHAPTER
22
The Shelter of God's Care

BARB'S DIARY, JANUARY 29, 1985:

I remember praying specifically that the publisher would be excited about The Door In the Dragon's Throat *and would be interested in working with Frank on additional books. Well, a letter indicated that they were anxious for the book to come out and are looking forward to reviewing any other work Frank may have. God hears our prayers! Praise His name!*

BARB'S DIARY, JANUARY 30, 1985:

Reading Psalm 73:28 this morning, I had to agree with David: "But it is good for me to draw near to God; I have put my trust in the Lord God, that I may declare all Your works."

What a blessing to be able to declare the works of God! He allowed Frank's children's

> *From the end of the earth I will cry to You, When my heart is overwhelmed; Lead me to the rock that is higher than I.*
>
> PSALM 61:2

book to be published! May our lives provide a living testimony of God's grace and provision as we are obedient to Him. Truly He has heard our supplications and has been a shelter in our times of trial.

The storm outside is moving on now. The hail and lightening have stopped and the thunder is growing distant. I pull the covers up to my chin, snuggling closer to Frank. The warmth from his body is so comfortable. I feel at peace and thank the Lord once again for His love and for providing shelter through yet another summer storm.

> *God's power and promise are a rock that is higher than we. This rock is Christ; these are safe that are in him.*
>
> MATTHEW HENRY

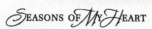

Frank and I both derive much pleasure from working in our yard. In fact, we've been known to quibble over who gets to mow the lawn! That may be because while accomplishing that task we can enjoy a 180-degree view of breathtaking serenity. But it's the grapevines entwining the arbor that leads to our courtyard that, as Frank says, "provide such fun even if we never get any grapes!" For three years Frank has pruned the living daylights out of them, and each year we've been amazed at their lush comeback.

During winter they look like nothing more than dead stubs poking up out of the ground. But in the spring, the little buds produce such a profusion of branches that we have to cut them back or there would be no fruit from the vines. So during the growing season, the branches are pruned back in order to direct all of the vine's energy toward producing fruit.

Each pruning season I am reminded how the Lord pruned us during one season of our spiritual growth. Though the outlook for our future showed no more promise than our pruned grapes do in winter, we did have the Lord's promise that if we would continue abiding in Him, our lives would eventually bear fruit pleasing to Him.

We had left the ministry due to burnout and were living at poverty level. But God did not forsake us. In an act of love, He sent friends to care for us. They brought us live chickens for eggs and meat, bought the cordwood we harvested from our property, and shared clothing with us that they had outgrown or no longer needed.

We didn't have much, but God always provided what we lacked from His surplus.

CHAPTER 23

Abiding in the Vine

BARB'S DIARY, JANUARY 29, 1985:

God has proved His faithfulness again and again. We didn't have the means with which to pay our bills but He provided:

- *Frank started a part-time job at the ski factory*

- *We sold $120.00 of firewood*

- *I found $5.00 in one of our pockets*

- *$6.00 came from returned gifts*

- *I received $130.00 for Christmas*

- *Frank will be paid for two upcoming speaking engagements*

- *We were given two large salmon and five pounds of cheese*

If not for the pruning we've been through these past several months, I might never have put so much trust in the Lord.

Our worldly possessions had been pruned away so our energies could be directed toward bearing spiritual fruit—fruit

Now in my prosperity I said, "I shall never be moved."

Psalm 30:6

that would endure. I cannot deny the pain that came with the pruning. It seemed that our very self-esteem lay cut to pieces on the garden floor. Frank and I had nothing to boast in—except the Cross of Christ our Lord. Had it not been for that one act of passion, our lives would seem worthless. But a life that derives its worth from the Lord is of great value indeed!

Even a smidgen of faith as insignificant as a tiny grapevine bud grows if it remains focused on the Vine. Yes, our spiritual lives will be pruned, but God promises that we will eventually bear fruit.

Ours was the enduring fruit of trust in a Savior who was faithfully and tenderly overseeing every detail of our lives.

Afflictions, though they seem severe, in mercy oft are sent.

Charles H. Spurgeon

69

Pain—the muscle cramps sharply from fatiguing repetition. A rivulet of sweat trickles down the skin. The body cries "NO MORE!" But the weight is lifted one more time. The hot muscle cramps, and throbbing pain surges up and down the limb. The muscle begins to shake and quiver—the weight has grown too heavy. Stressed beyond its limit, the muscle fails.

Body builders call this "the good fail." I learned about it when I started to read and gather information about weight lifting. At the time, I was experiencing severe muscle tension and Frank had developed a strained muscle in his hand from signing books, playing the banjo, and working at his computer. After treatments with a physical therapist, we both began to work out in a gym to strengthen our muscles and relieve tautness. I quickly began to identify with "the good fail."

That term also had spiritual signifi-

CHAPTER 24

The "Good Fail"

cance for us during the seemingly non-ending months of financially lean times. After Frank left his position as an associate pastor, we continued to end up with more month than money. Merely meeting our daily living expenses widened the hole in our pockets. Though we seriously sought God's guidance, we found ourselves without permanent employment. Our faith was pushed to the limit as we counted every penny and made every penny count.

Trying to spend our money wisely forced us to make every decision carefully: should we spend money on gas or should we purchase bath tissue? I found a recipe for cold cereal and baked several batches so Frank could enjoy a bowl for breakfast now and then.

I felt as though my emotions were being pushed almost to a breaking point. As though forging our faith with repetitious challenges, God tried us daily and proved us. He forced us through the stress and strain to place our faith in Him. We needed to feel the pain that built our faith so God could make us strong in Him.

During this time, we were raising chickens. My sister had given us an incubator for Christmas, and we delighted in watching the little chicks hatch, struggling out of their shells. They would peck with their beaks, strain with their legs, struggle and fail, and then strain some more. Our sympathy for them overwhelmed us at times. We wanted to chip away bits of shell to help the poor, weak chicks break free. But, of course, we didn't dare do that. It would have made the chicks weak. In order to be strong, they need the struggling and failing and struggling again. It

It is good for me that I have been afflicted, that I may learn Your statutes.

PSALM 119:71

Worldly ease is a great foe to faith; it loosens the joints of holy valor and snaps the sinews of sacred courage.

CHARLES H. SPURGEON

builds their muscles for the life ahead.

What a parable was being played out before us. Just as God planned to strengthen the chicks by allowing them to struggle out of their shells, so He had planned to strengthen us spiritually by allowing us to face struggles in our lives.

Reflecting on those little chicks challenges my faith. When a difficult struggle comes my way, I pray I will have the strength to lift the weight one more rep or, like the chicks, to keep struggling even against formidable circumstances. It's "the good spiritual fail." And we all need the struggles from time to time to strengthen our spiritual muscles.

By 1985, Frank and I were approaching our early- to mid-thirties. And though we had walked with the Lord all our lives, it seemed that our continuing meager lifestyle brought clarity to Jesus' statement, "except you become as little children." The poverty that loomed over us daily not only demonstrated our frail mortality, but proved that we needed a heavenly Father— One who knew our despairing predicaments and would use our insufficiency to prove his fatherly love.

BARB'S DIARY, FEBRUARY 11, 1985:

Even though it's been a test of faith, Frank and I are beginning to understand that just as children learn to trust their earthly father we've had to learn to trust our heavenly Father to care for all our needs—which He has done in His own curious way.

Whenever food or supplies fall short, money or friends arrive to fill the lack:

A family from our church brought a Christmas gift basket. Two large steaks and potatoes they gave stretched into four meals. From small loaves of cheese and salami that were tucked into that same basket God multiplied pizza for three additional meals.

More friends shared their freshly caught salmon, providing two evenings of sumptuous dining.

The prolific outlay of eggs from our chickens made quiche and omelets common fare, and one of our roosters became four dinners of chicken and dumplings.

Our garden has kept us well supplied with vegetables. We've eaten fresh leeks and chard all through winter along with frozen or canned green beans, cauliflower, pickles, and beets. Our lettuce slowed its production in mid-November so we began adding swiss chard or chickweed to our salads. We've made soup from vegetable stock and dried food items on hand.

Our February property payment was due,

CHAPTER
25
Faith
as a
Child

but Frank's check from the ski factory wasn't expected until later in the month. I figured that for the first time in twelve and a half years of marriage, we'd be late with the payment. I should be ashamed of myself! Unexpectedly, Frank was paid for his first three days of work! Combining the paycheck with a speaking honorarium enabled us to make our payment on time!

I've felt like the Israelites collecting manna in the wilderness. At the right time and in the exact amount, the LORD provides no more and no less. This has truly made life a daily walk of faith! Praise Him for His goodness.

It's the natural inclination. When we are desperate we call out to God, but when we are enjoying prosperity we don't see the need. From our own experiences, Frank and I have learned to act otherwise. Even when we enjoy a prosperous season we still find life punctuated by desperate circumstances that require a daily walk of faith. There are still many times when our understanding of God's work in our lives is not clear. We have to live each day with only the knowledge that He has granted us.

Whether Frank and I are in desperate circumstances or in prosperity, when our finite knowledge is stretched to the limits of our understanding we are reminded to become as little children, trusting every detail of our lives to the care of our heavenly Father.

> *As children, we must be careful for nothing, but leave it to our heavenly Father to care for us. As children are little in body and low in stature, so we must be little and low in spirit, and in our thoughts of ourselves. . . . The age of childhood is the learning age.*
>
> MATTHEW HENRY

> *Therefore whoever humbles himself as this little child is the greatest in the kingdom of heaven.*
>
> MATTHEW 18:4

Frank flourished with every opportunity to write, but his writing nearly withered while he was employed building skis. From our perspective, we were headed for another drought!

Frank obediently took the job God had provided at the ski factory, but sitting in the car in the early morning darkness as I drove him to work, we routinely petitioned the Lord, *"Please send us showers of blessings."*

Building skis was not Frank's first choice, but it did provide an income. And though Frank didn't have much time to spend on writing, the story kept brewing in his heart. So at odd moments here and there he kept writing. He was compelled to write the story, even if it never got published!

FRANK'S DIARY:

"I don't know if I'll ever get The Heavenlies *sold. I may end up shelving it for good!"*

We searched though the fiction section of our local Christian bookstore and were not very encouraged. All we discovered was a rather desolate wasteland of publishers in this new type of fiction. That meant there were probably not many publishers out there who would be willing to risk such a project. Yet because of the Lord's gentle prodding, Frank kept pursuing the idea.

By September 1984, Frank had compiled a two-page synopsis. He sent the synopsis and a few exhilarating scenes from the book to several publishers. We prayed that at least one proposal would bring the promise of rain.

Sure enough, on October twenty-second, Crossway Books trickled a bit of optimism onto our hopelessness. They wanted to see a complete manuscript of *The Heavenlies*. And it hadn't even been written!

My mother, always supportive of our efforts, enthusiastically volunteered her typing skills. So she and I pounded away on the final draft. Meanwhile, invigorated by the news, Frank brandished his shorthand and began swashbuckling his way through the concluding fight scene.

On November twenty-six at 8:04 p.m. Frank placed the final period at the end of the final sentence and pronounced, *"It's done!"* It

CHAPTER 26

Showers of Rain

> *Ask you of the Lord rain. Do not pray to the clouds, nor to the stars for rain, but to the Lord; for He it is who hears the heavens, when they hear the earth.*
>
> MATTHEW HENRY

pen, we threw caution to the wind and indulged . . . in a lavish banana split at the local Dairy Queen!

As the final draft took shape at our typewriters, an excitement electrified the air. Was it possible that we were part of a divine appointment? Driven by the prospect of some long-awaited "rain," we photocopied 750 pages of manuscript and on December fourth laid out eight dollars and forty-five cents for first class postage. We mailed it to Crossway Books in an old church bulletin box.

BARB'S DIARY, DECEMBER 20, 1985:

Every day rotates around the mailbox.

January, nothing. February, silence. Weeks languished into March . . . the thunderclouds

was the fulfillment of a dream, the culmination of a burden that had driven Frank relentlessly until that moment.

Although we could barely afford the ink in Frank's

seem to be vanishing on the horizon.

But finally, a perpetually prayed-over, long-awaited, much-desired shower arrived, and Frank was home to welcome it!

BARB'S DIARY, MARCH 25, 1985:

Crossway Books wants to publish <u>The Heavenlies</u>! They couldn't put it down; they read it in two days! A summer 1986 release is planned. The phone call promised a contract with a $1,000.00 advance to follow!

There were tears, hallelujahs, and praises to the Lord. We were dancing for joy! Drenched with thankfulness, we savored the news over a fine Mexican meal and reminisced over the long, difficult years when we had waited for this "rain."

Because it would be a year before his novel was published and some time before we would receive any royalties, Frank continued to work at the ski factory. It didn't matter to us now. The thunderclouds rumbled in the distance with the promise of rain, and there was hope that Frank would someday become a flourishing writer!

> *Ask the LORD for rain*
> *In the time of the latter rain.*
> *The LORD will make flashing clouds;*
> *He will give them showers of rain,*
> *Grass in the field for everyone.*
>
> ZECHARIAH 10:1

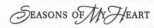

Frank hasn't worked in three weeks, and my schedule at work may be shortened several days. I feel panic coming over me, but the Lord reminds me, He'll take care of our needs.

The news that Frank's manuscript was to be published rejuvenated us but offered no long-term, and certainly no immediate, solution to our failing finances and sagging dispositions. Though Frank was working intermittently building skis and I was working part-time as an orthodontist's assistant, we had no choice that year but to pay our taxes with a bankcard check.

Not only had we run short of money, we were running out of options, running out of ideas, and running short on hope. Things simply *had* to get better!

Now in debt to the IRS, Frank had no choice but to continue working at the ski factory he had been so glad to leave ten years ago. He was despondent that things would never change for him. His dreams of writing full time lay far beyond the factory, and he desperately needed some assurance that those dreams would not die.

"We need hope, Lord!"

About that time, for some unknown reason, the manager moved Frank from his edge-routing job for a few days and placed him alone to side-paint a mountain of skis. Depressed with life and ungrateful for the work, Frank used the freedom of his solitude to engage in a long, loud list of "I wants."

I want a better home.

I want to live more comfortably.

I want to be a better provider.

I want to get out of the factory!!!

After releasing his pent-up frustrations out loud, Frank conceded that perhaps he had expected too much, too fast. In the quiet of the room, he began to reflect on all the ways that God had provided for us and cared for us. Slowly he became overwhelmed with the grace of God's abundant love. Frank's heart was touched deeply and a river of tears

CHAPTER 27

Resting in God

For I know the thoughts that I think toward you, says the LORD, thoughts of peace and not of evil, to give you a future and a hope.

JEREMIAH 29:11

coursed down his cheeks. Releasing emotions from his innermost being, he repented of his temporal values and unappreciative attitudes. When all was exhausted, what remained was a sincere, empty vessel now vulnerable to God's gentle, merciful healing.

"Lord, I trust you. I'm yours."

And then as if being held in the very hands of God, a divine peace came over Frank. He felt God speaking to him, almost in an audible voice:

"Take no thought for your immediate needs; know that I will care for you. My love lies deep and intimate; I will never leave you. As for the future, I have plans that will fulfill your deepest desires and bring purpose and meaning to all you have been through . . . but for now, just rest in My arms."

Overcome by the magnitude of God's loving concern for us, Frank recorded these thoughts in his journal:

"I feel such a wonderful assurance that

God has some remarkable things planned, as if my stories and creativity will touch millions and become things that endure."

If I were dealing with a man's promise, I should carefully consider the ability and the character of the man who had covenanted with me. So with the promise of God; my eye must not be so much fixed upon the greatness of the mercy—that may stagger me—as upon the greatness of the promiser—that will cheer me.

CHARLE H. SPURGEON
MORNING AND EVENING

A time of hope, so gracious and dear, unburdened a season when life lay heavily upon us. In a fragile moment God dismantled despair, and the comfort Frank received those few days never deserted him. Even now, when he experiences doubt, just recalling those compassionate moments will cause Frank to weep as he senses that God is still holding him, still reminding him:

"For now . . . just rest in My arms."

For You are my hope, O Lord GOD; You are my trust from my youth.

PSALM 71:5

81

A stray cat patiently peered through our French door, waiting, hoping that we would adopt her. She paid us a visit every day. She did not know us, and we did not know her; yet, she hoped in what did not exist: a relationship with us. In the end, through sustaining perseverance, her hope became reality—we opened the French door and welcomed her into our hearts and our home. It was an object lesson to me of Romans 8:24–25: "Hope that is seen is not hope; for why does one still hope for what he sees? But if we hope for what we do not see, we eagerly wait for it with perseverance."

Why *not* patiently hope in what we do not see? At this point in our lives our very faith hinged on that concept.

Frank's part-time job edge-routing snow skis freed his mind to formulate fictitious characters into page-turning plots—plots he hoped would eventually support a full-time writing career. *And why not hope?*

Wasn't it only months ago that he'd prayed for a publisher and now had two novels due for release?

Frank's fingers fairly flew over his typewriter. Hesitating only occasionally, he kept time with the pileated woodpecker visiting the old nag outside our cabin. Peck, peck. Stop. Peck-peck-peck-peck-peck-peck. It was not Frank's usual slow, type-a-few-words-and-pause method of writing. He was writing "Tilly," a radio drama.

For months he worked a few days building skis, then a few days writing "Tilly." In his mind he listened to our friends' voices, then chose actors based on the sound of their voice. Jury-rigging a studio in our 8-by-24-foot trailer, Frank clipped microphones to hanging blankets. This muffled extraneous sounds and provided tents in which the cast recorded their lines. When the drama captured the message to Frank's satisfaction, he mixed the voices with background

CHAPTER 28

Hope That Is Seen Is Not Hope

sounds, then carried the master cassette to a local Christian radio station.

"Sorry, Frank. Radio dramas are a thing of the past!"

Undaunted, after weeks of perseverance, "Tilly" was broadcast throughout Seattle on Sanctity of Life Sunday in 1986. Soon stations across the country aired "Tilly," and listeners began to mail copies of the drama to Focus On the Family.

One and a half years later, amid a din of nearly 200 blaring boom boxes, Frank leaned closer to his own radio. Listening, he felt a thrill of excitement. Dr. James Dobson was enthusiastically introducing "Tilly," a Focus On the Family premier reenactment of the original radio drama written by Mr. Frank Peretti!

Surrounded by cold concrete walls and outfitted in his denim apron,

Hope itself is like a star—not to be seen in the sunshine of prosperity, and only to be discovered in the night of adversity.

CHARLES H. SPURGEON

I have set the LORD always before me; Because He is at my right hand I shall not be moved. Therefore my heart is glad, and my glory rejoices; My flesh also will rest in hope.

PSALM 16:8–9

geek safety glasses, rubber gloves, and sneakers, that same "Mr. Frank Peretti" (somewhat distracted today from filling his daily quota) carefully but quickly slopped resin into a ski mold. *Curioclipse* is Frank's word to describe that moment on August 10, 1987: Amidst 300 factory workers, in a noisy manufacturing plant, one lone ski maker's mere *hope* vicariously reached beyond the factory walls and became a tool in the hands of God.

It began as nothing more than a hope, yet Frank did not deviate from the course God had set for him. Because of Frank's perseverance in a proven faith, God still uses "Tilly" today to touch thousands of lives. Frank's hope in that which was not seen has become a life-giving reality.

God *is* faithful to His word.

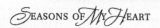

The job at K2, the ski factory, did help us get back on our feet financially, but like reading a slow book, Frank just wanted to get on with the next chapter. He wanted to write. So he took a six-month assignment on weekend-shift in order to clear his weekday schedule.

FRANK'S JOURNAL, AUGUST 12, 1986:

It seems nothing comes easy. Maybe the Lord is trying to strengthen my resolve. I have to try my best and either succeed or fail, but I can't quit writing.

I feel like some guy scratching, clawing, desperately climbing out of a pit: Freedom and fulfillment are above me, the devouring lion of K2 below. My choice: Either keep scratching and clawing to get something else going or settle for working at K2 the rest of my life. With that thought, it's easy to see quitting is not an option!

With strengthened resolve, Frank scratched and clawed at his writing. By the summer of 1986 he had three kids' novels in print, and *The Heavenlies* was released under its published title, *This Present Darkness*. It wasn't long before the recurring comment about that book was, "It's selling like hotcakes!" By August 1987, 30,000 copies were in print.

Though Frank felt bound to the factory, what God accomplished beyond those walls soon opened new doors: his audio drama "Tilly" began getting airplay across the country—which stimulated radio interviews, which led to more speaking engagements!

FRANK'S JOURNAL, SEPTEMBER 21, 1987:

I think my ministry is growing so quickly I'm going to need some good professional help.

Frank accepted a timely offer with a firm that would begin managing his career. Simultaneously, Crossway proposed a contract for *Piercing the Darkness*, offering

CHAPTER
29
The End of a Chapter

> *Good words will not do without good works. We must abound in good works, and in every good work: not in some only which are more easy, and suitable, and safe, but in all, and every instance of them.*
>
> MATTHEW HENRY

$1,000-per-month advance. Coupling that with speaking honorariums would free Frank to leave the factory.

FRANK'S JOURNAL, JANUARY 13, 1988:

Today is my 37th birthday; I'm feeling very pensive about how far I've come. With all that has developed over the last three years, I feel I'm finally starting the life the Lord has been preparing me for.

FRANK'S JOURNAL, JANUARY 21, 1988:

Today was my last day at K2, a very bittersweet moment, almost unreal. It'll take a while to get used to the idea I'm really out of there. People in the pressroom made me a cake and signed a ski for me, a nice surprise.

So . . . on the night of January 21, Barb picked me up, and I walked out the K2 doors for the last time. God answered prayer, and accomplished His purpose. Praise His Name!

Though working in the factory had been frustrating for Frank, God used it to mold his frustration into a strengthened resolve that has been vital to his writing career. Sometimes we have to endure a seemingly slow and unbearable season in life before we're ready to get on with the next chapter.

Propped near the computer where Frank writes is the ski his co-workers signed. Good-bye sentiments written in permanent ink have become even more meaningful over time: "Good luck, I'll read your books." "Enjoy your life." "Guess this is the end of a chapter!"

It literally was the end of a chapter, and with God's purpose fulfilled, a whole new season was about to unfold.

> *It is God who works in you both to will and to do for His good pleasure.*
>
> PHILIPPIANS 2:13

> *And we know that all things work together for good to those who love God, to those who are the called according to His purpose.*
>
> ROMANS 8:28

And he shall be like a tree planted by the rivers of water, that bringeth forth his fruit in his season (Ps. 1:3).

A tree flourishing by the water was not the picture of Frank when he returned to the ski factory in January 1985. I watched him through thirteen years of struggle as he ambled through those doors. But by 1988 we realized those thirteen years had rooted our faith in Jesus. Now, as rivers of grace rose and strengthened our weary hearts, opportunities began to unfold like clouds of cherry blossoms promising a fruitful season.

FRANK'S JOURNAL, JANUARY 11, 1988:

The Lord has continued to move, doing all things well, in their place and in their season.

It was as if all the years of struggling, hoping, and believing in God's promises had accumulated behind some heavenly dam and the floodgates were finally opened, pouring blessings upon us.

Frank now had contracts for "Tilly" and

CHAPTER
30
Planted by Rivers of Water

Piercing the Darkness. While he wrote, his managers worked with a promotional team to schedule bookstore and media tours, and a speaker's bureau began handling the speaking engagements that now took Frank far beyond Seattle into the rest of the country.

Other publishers began offering book contracts, larger organizations wanted to hear Frank speak, and several people in the film industry talked of making *This Present Darkness* into a movie. The invigorating book sales and nationwide interest in Frank's speaking revived our struggling existence.

BARB'S DIARY, NOVEMBER 8, 1988:

This Present Darkness sold 7,000 copies in February, 8,000 in March, 44,000 in August, and over 40,000 in October! Whoopie!!

Distributors were marketing it, pastors were plugging it, singers were promoting it. A college dean made it a course prerequisite, and in Christian schools it was required reading.

BARB'S DIARY, NOVEMBER 28, 1988:

I want to go on record saying that even though Frank's book has become a "best-seller" we know it's because God ordained it and must realize this is a season and things will change. Our happiness must be rooted in the Lord and not dependent on book sales or media attention. Circumstances change; God doesn't.

BARB'S DIARY, JUNE 24, 1989:

It is expected from those who enjoy the mercies of grace that, both in the temper of their minds and in the tenor of their lives, . . . they bring forth fruit. And, be it observed to the praise of the great dresser of the vineyard, they bring forth their fruit (that which is required of them) in due season, when it is most beautiful and most useful, improving every opportunity of doing good and doing it in its proper time.

MATTHEW HENRY

Today is our 17th anniversary. Frank and I feel a special warmth and happiness in this season. It's marvelous to look back and see how the LORD has been with us all these years.

God has poured out a blessing

we cannot contain! May we continually hear from Him and follow His leading.

By July 1989 *This Present Darkness* had sold 500,000 copies; *Piercing The Darkness* sold 300,000 before it even reached the bookstores. *This Present Darkness* was named number one on the Best-Seller Paperback Fiction list for 1988, and in October 1989 both books had one million copies in print.

Such strong sales figures and exciting opportunities could have swept us away in the wrong direction, but our faith, deeply rooted from so many years of struggle, helped us keep our eyes firmly on the Lord. Instead, the strong sales and new opportunities clearly indicated to us that Frank's writing and speaking were making a cultural impact and affecting lives.

There was fruit.

Our season had come at last.

Along the bank of the river . . . will grow all kinds of trees used for food. . . . They will bear fruit every month, because their water flows from the sanctuary.
EZEKIEL 47:12

"You must be Frank Peretti's wife . . . oh . . . I'm sorry . . . you probably get tired of hearing that. How do you prefer to be identified?"

"As Frank's wife!" I responded gladly.

Being a wife and homemaker may not be glamorous, but from an early age that was my only desire. Finally, in 1989, when Frank's writing career was established, I counted it a privilege to be able to come home and find fulfillment in those roles. But for fifteen years I felt trapped:

BARB'S DIARY, DECEMBER 28, 1981:

I've quit my job. I just can't continue working, being a homemaker, and a wife. It's too stressful! My prayer and Frank's is that someday his writing and speaking will become our sole source of support.

My job at the insurance agency greeted me every morning with a huge stack of files needing my attention. Each file, representing a client's needs, required several hours of reading, comparative shopping, telephoning, completing forms, and accurately quoting premiums. My stomach churned with each ring of the telephone. It meant that I had to drop whatever I was doing, take the call, open another file, and add it to my stack. My desk was buried under manuals, forms, files, and charts. I felt like I was sinking in a quagmire of paperwork. I just couldn't get ahead of the game! . . . I wanted to be at home with my husband.

Occasionally, when I did quit work, we endured some financially fret-filled seasons as we sought the Lord for His direction. I mended the holes in Frank's socks again and again, and if not for loving friends we might never have had new clothes. Lentil burgers became a weekly staple, and firewood was our sole source of heat.

Had I decided to work full time, material things might have come more easily. But God had placed a mandate on my life that

> *Who can find a virtuous wife? For her worth is far above rubies. The heart of her husband safely trusts her; so he will have no lack of gain. She does him good and not evil all the days of her life.*
>
> PROVERBS 31:10–12

even poverty could not destroy. That mandate—my heart's desire—was to be Frank's wife.

BARB'S DIARY, NOVEMBER 8, 1982:

God is showing me something new about "being Frank's wife." By staying home, praying, and inviting God to fill this place with His peace and joy, our home will become a refuge where God can minister to Frank in ways I never could. Maybe it's because of Frank's desire to serve the Lord that I feel this so strongly. Perhaps the Lord wants me home cultivating an environment from which a ministry can grow.

Learning to trust God rather than myself eventually set Frank and me free to become all God wanted us to be. Since I no longer walked in the door carrying the burdens of my workday, a new peace accompanied our lives.

Now one of the greatest and most cherished rewards of being a full-time wife and homemaker comes in moments when Frank looks at me with an expression that steals my heart and takes my breath away. His eyes sparkle and his smile says, "I cherish you, and I want to be with you always." I blush, dropping my eyes . . . but in those moments I smile and think, *"I'm free to be his wife!"*

> *A good woman will be a good wife and make it her business to please her husband. Though she is a woman of spirit herself, yet her desire is to her husband, to know his mind, that she may accommodate herself to it. She is a good wife who is fit to be trusted, and he is a good husband who will leave it to such a wife to manage for him.*
>
> MATTHEW HENRY

"THIS IS THE MOST TEDIOUS JOB IN THE WORLD!" cried a young construction worker as he slathered pallets of sloppy stucco onto the sides of our new home. Frank and I laughingly concurred, knowing all too well that some jobs are definitely "the most tedious"!

Mundane routine can be quite boring, yet hidden there we discover tools that are useful in assisting us through the three score and ten years allotted us. From 1972 to 1988 Frank and I were involved in numerous occupations that were tedious to us, yet they produced underlying lessons that are relevant to so many aspects of our lives today.

CHAPTER 32
Growing Through the Mundane

As Sunday school teachers we learned the Bible. As a variety store clerk and a print shop employee we learned servanthood. In insurance I learned problem solving and organization. As a musician and writers we have learned that practice makes you do whatever you do better. And in the pastorate we learned patience, mercy, and grace.

Years of work at a ski factory reminded Frank daily that there were other things he wanted to do with the rest of his life! Surrounded by featureless, cement walls, high fluorescent lighting, and radios blaring a wild assortment of rock music was not something he thrived on. But one thing he did learn from slopping resin into ski molds, painting the sides of the skis, and sanding ski bases was that the job provided a steady income. It kept food on the table and the bills paid. It was dependable work that God had supplied to meet our needs.

Frank always had a desire to write, but it took thirty-three years of life, some schooling, and several jobs before he sold his first manuscript. Today the underlying lessons he learned from the daily routines of life provide the grist for a large portion of his writing. Learning to cope with different personality traits is daily routine, but combining those personalities into characters of fiction converts the mundane into exciting ingredients for novels. Feeling frustration when a plan goes awry is routine, but weaving those obstructions into a story that people can relate to creates a new treasure from daily routine.

Old experiences, and new observations, all have their use; and we must not content ourselves with old discoveries, but must be adding new. Live and learn.

MATTHEW HENRY

The education never ends. So when you think you can't bear to repeat another day of the "same old, same old," just ask yourself, *"What new treasure can I glean from the same old routine? How can I perceive the tedious in a new and different way?"*

Frank and I enjoy turning what may be mundane for others into something a little fun. Our postmaster enjoys a joke and bears up well under our teasing. I've even left cookies at the bottom of the driveway to cheer her day. I have had candy delivered to the snowplow crew, and enjoy opportunities to return grocery carts for weary shoppers. After our shop was built we delivered truckloads of "mundane" dirt to our neighbors to fill an area where their new shop now stands!

Now may the God of peace . . . make you complete in every good work to do His will, working in you what is well pleasing in His sight, through Jesus Christ. . . .

HEBREWS 13:20–21

Gold is mined from rock. Maturity is mined from the fertile veins of the tedious and mundane. Seasoned maturity can yield such precious prizes as patience, understanding, wisdom, knowledge, mercy, and grace. These are indestructible treasures we can glean to enrich the lives of those around us.

What a difference a few short years make! Entries from my 1989–91 diary begin

Frank is in LA for a few days . . .

We flew to Orlando . . .

Frank is in Chicago taping . . .

We flew to Europe . . .

Frank is in Baltimore, his first night on tour . . .

Tomorrow we leave for Estes Park . . .

We'll be going to Washington D.C., then on to Denver . . .

Frank flies to Canada tomorrow . . .

We'll fly to Nashville then on to Virginia and Washington D.C. . . .

Our life was suddenly transformed from calm and predictable to exciting and hectic. We desperately needed to find a balance between the two!

When Frank finished writing *Prophet*, in 1992, his time became consumed with

CHAPTER 33
The Backside of the Mountain

speaking engagements, interviews, magazine articles, manuscript reviews, short stories, and books on tape. His photo appeared in dozens of newspapers and magazines, and he completed dozens more television and radio interviews—"How does it feel to be 'king of Christian fiction' with millions of books in print?"

We were greeted at the airport in luxury cars and limousines, while at home our 1979 Mustang was on its last legs and we still lived in our 8-by-24-foot travel trailer. It seemed that Christendom was painting a bigger-than-life picture of Frank Peretti, and we grew uncomfortable with the pedestal we felt ourselves teetering on. Though the gestures were kind and the attention positive, we still needed to keep a sober view of life, to hone a discerning ear that would hear the Lord's voice above all the others that were vying for our attention.

While seeking God's direction in all our ventures, one thing we have always tried to protect is a quiet, secluded lifestyle. Yet

The most active servants of Christ cannot be always upon the stretch of business, but have bodies that require some relaxation, some breathing-time. . . . Let but proper time be set, and kept for everything, and a great deal of work may be done with a great deal of ease. But if people be continually coming and going, and no rule or method be observed, a little work will not be done without a deal of trouble.

MATTHEW HENRY

defending and preserving that portion of our life was becoming more and more complex. Just when life seemed to be speeding furiously away from what we held dear, the Lord helped us to slow down our pace.

In 1992 we found a home and acreage tucked into a hillside at the end of a road in Northern Idaho. We felt immediate peace in the quiet surroundings and knew this was where we wanted to live. It is a place far removed from the hubbub of humanity where, alone in the quiet company of the Lord, we can gain a proper perspective to our daily endeavors. A walk up our old logging road always brings a fresh outlook as graceful osprey soar on warm summer breezes of sweet-smelling pine. And resting on a large, warm rock surrounded by wild daisies we can enjoy a panorama of mountains illuminated in the setting sun—a wonderful spot for a moment of unspoiled meditation!

When our entanglements with this world begin to obscure God's directives, our private retreat provides a place where we can sort out the busyness that surrounds us. My girlfriend calls this, "living on the backside of the mountain"—a sentiment that aptly describes our cozy home, tucked into a hillside at the end of a road.

"Living on the backside of a mountain" provides an interlude from demanding schedules, a place where season by season, through life's mountains and valleys, we find a peaceful seclusion from the sometimes wild and wearying world. It offers relief from the exciting and hectic. It brings a balance we *all* need.

And He said to them, "Come aside by yourselves to a deserted place and rest a while." For there were many coming and going. . . . So they departed to a deserted place in the boat by themselves.

MARK 6:31–32

"I have called you friends." Jesus said. And later He added, "Come and dine."

Those words invoke such a gracious welcome. Frank and I extended that same invitation one Sunday in August, 1996. Our cherished and closest friends from two distinct seasons of our lives were uniting at our home for baptism, dinner, music, and fellowship.

Some of those friends had helped to sustain us during our turbulent season of the '80s. They had just spent the week with us floating the river, fishing, and sharing meals while reminiscing over the years when we became fibers woven into each other's lives.

More recent friends, whose lives were now being entwined with ours, added new texture to the day. Other friends from the band Frank plays in planned an after-dinner concert, and our pastor and his family added their warmth and friendship. Last but not least were our Wednesday night dinner-and-Bible-study companions (and the illustrators for this book) Rick and Carrie Parks. Several months earlier they had set aside this day to be baptized in the river below our home.

Actually, four people were going to be baptized, testifying of their love for the Lord. Four more fibers would be woven into the fabric of God's eternal plan, four more souls responding to that divine call, "come and dine." Their silhouetted images, surrounded by the jeweled sunshine that reflected off tiny waves at the river's edge, created a striking focal point. The picture was completed by the touching testimonies of these who had "died" to their old way of life and were "raised" to newness of life. Sweet sentiments spoken in warm embraces, and endearing fellowship secured because of our love for the Lord, framed those sacred moments, now forever captured in our memories.

CHAPTER 34

Friends Meeting Friends

Finally, it was time to "come and *dine*." Heaps of barbecued chicken, ribs, potatoes, baked beans, and corn-on-the-cob, garnished with laughter and great stories, made the meal an absolute feast not only for our bodies but also for our souls!

After dinner we settled on blankets, and the group, Northern Cross, enlivened the afternoon with their energetic music. In the vista beyond, sparkling blue waters meandered through the valley below as late afternoon rays from the setting sun emblazoned the foothills of the Rockies.

After the concert ended we moved from the cool summer evening outside into the cozy ambiance of our warm living room. A young friend who at the age of eleven had played "Tilly" in our original radio drama was

Get nearer to Jesus, and you will find yourself linked more and more in spirit to all who are like yourself, supported by the same heavenly manna. If we were more near to Jesus, we should be more near to one another.

CHARLES H. SPURGEON
MORNING AND EVENING

You are My friends if you do whatever I command you. . . . I have called you friends, for all things that I heard from My Father I have made known to you.

JOHN 15:14–15

now "great with child" herself. She stood near her husband, seated at the piano, and the two of them enchanted us with a duet. Another friend who played the cello accompanied a piano recital, and other friends shared songs from their hearts. The hours slipped away as our souls grew together in sweet rapport.

"Come and dine." Friends meeting friends, lives intertwining, souls being knit together—each individual a single thread creatively woven into a day rich in memories. Fellowship, holy baptism, and a congenial repast patterned one more golden day in the magnificent tapestry of our lives.

Two very special worlds converged that day as we basked in intimate camaraderie. Friends. *Friends, in the Lord*. Without them our lives would never be the same.

I will always consider it an act of love that Frank moved us back to my birthplace, adding new memories to the ones I had accumulated in the Idaho mountains with my family. Those memories were such a help to me when we suddenly found ourselves gathered in Mom's kitchen—without Dad. Those dark days, blurred behind a veil of painful tears, were interwoven with tender reminiscing over fond memories of our beloved father, our hero.

That dreaded day had come without warning. It had come too soon. No, God's timing is perfect, . . . right? That's what I had always believed . . . but then, I wasn't sure. It was difficult to reason.

There were so many papers to sign, so many decisions to make. What kind of coffin did we want? What about his wedding ring? "Here are the clothes Paul was wearing, would you like them?" *Perhaps there is a lingering scent we can capture for those often-lonely moments?*

CHAPTER 35

Dad's Passing

Harsh words stabbed my emotions: death, burial, coffin, grave clothes. *Lord, I hate having to think about these things!* I wanted to hide, to collect my thoughts.

"Tell me something about Paul for the obituary." How can you be brief about your champion? There were so many memories of our Idaho adventures: dinner picnics at the lake, boating, weekends at the cabin he'd built. His smile! We were always greeted with that incredible smile.

My father's hat lay on the chair in my parent's bedroom, pocket items strewn across his dresser. Everything lay untouched since his hand had placed them there. Now he would never be back to use them. Mom would have to decide what would become of them.

People said Dad was "bigger than life." Now my good friend, counselor, and hero had suddenly vanished from life! I would never get to hug him, laugh with him, or hear his stories and receive his advice

again here on earth. Was he taken too soon? As I reasoned in my bed those solitary nights, I finally came to my conclusion. That Sunday, March 12th, 1995, when God's finger stopped Dad's aortic valve, in His sovereign and unique design for our lives, it was *exactly* the right time.

Colorful images illumined those darkened days. Images of Dad in heaven laughing with the sons and daughters who were lost before birth. I imagined him singing to them, being the father they had never known. I clung to these thoughts through the dreariness like a rainbow through the rain, promising that heaven will be a wondrous place.

O Joy, that seekest me through pain,
I dare not close my eyes to thee.
I trace the rainbow through the rain.
And feel the promise is not vain,
That morn shall tearless be.

GEORGE MATHESON
"O LOVE THAT WILL NOT LET ME GO"

If in this life only we have hope
in Christ, we are of all men the
most pitiable. But now Christ
is risen from the dead, and has
become the firstfruits of those
who have fallen asleep.

1 CORINTHIANS 15:19–20

I expect that my remarkable father, my wise counselor, and devoted friend awaits the arrival of the rest of his family. And a Heavenly Father, a wiser counselor, a dearer friend and Savior also waits. Jesus' resurrection conquered death, extending to us life eternal and the promise of an incredible reunion where joy eternal will replace all earthly sorrow.

Though tears still fall occasionally, I am comforted in knowing that one day I will be reunited with my Dad and my Heavenly Father, who has promised to wipe away those tears—for with Him life eternal will forever tearless be.

Traditionally, my father asked the blessing over our evening meal and then consistently repeated one phrase: *"We thank you Father for all that we have, for all that we have comes from Thee."*

I will never forget that phrase, for in twenty-five years of marriage, the Lord has reminded us that, assuredly, "all that we have" has come from Him. Our experience with poverty in the '70s and '80s taught us to be thankful for God's provision. A half-gallon of milk, a tank of gas, firewood for the stove—all were gifts from heaven that we depended on daily.

Between 1990 and 1992, though, God began opening the windows of heaven and pouring out blessings we could hardly contain. We moved from our trailer with the shack around it to a large log home in the mountains. Purchasing milk and gas didn't seem quite as expensive now, and we owned 120 acres of firewood. Truly "our barns were filled with plenty and

our presses were bursting with new wine" (Proverbs 3:10).

But in the wake of the country's economic instability, it wasn't long before prophecy teachers and financial advisors began mapping out strategic plans for protecting one's worldly assets. While Frank and I were thankful for the abundance God had provided, a foreboding monster of economic paranoia began lurking in the shadows, stalking us with its tentacles of anxiety. Our "barns filled with plenty" now posed a new dilemma: *"Who owned what? Did we own our possessions, or did our possessions own us?"*

As my girlfriend and I walked our four-mile trek to the post office and back, we discussed how we might prepare for an economic crash. We could store grain, stock our pantries, grow our vegetables, and raise some chickens. I shared with her what Frank and I had been hearing: "Buy gold, it's easily negotiable and universally

CHAPTER
36

All That
We Have
Comes
From Thee

accepted"; "invest in overseas stocks"; "set up foreign bank accounts." After listening to this advice, she slowed the pace of our walk, turned thoughtfully, and remarked, "That's really great if you can *do* that sort of thing. I guess all our family can do is to put our trust in the Lord."

My mouth dropped open, and words caught in my throat. I looked at her . . . then out of delight I laughed. Her words had identified precisely where our focus belonged!

Franks says we had our kingdoms mixed up. Our eyes were so focused on loosing God's *provision* that we had forgotten to trust

The more men have, the more perplexity they have with it, and the more solicitous they are to keep what they have and to add to it, how to spare, and how to spend. So that even the abundance of the rich will not suffer them to sleep, for thinking what they shall do with what they have and how they shall dispose of it.

MATTHEW HENRY

Oh, taste and see that the LORD is good; Blessed is the man who trusts in Him! Oh, fear the LORD, you His saints! There is no want to those who fear Him.

PSALM 34:8–9

the *Provider*. It doesn't matter what our net worth is or what we've stored up for the future. The point is that when God's people are in need, He fills the lack. In the '80s He actually delivered groceries to our door!

Now when the paranoia of economic anxiety comes stalking, I prioritize my "kingdoms." I take my eyes off the "barns filled with plenty" and place my trust in the Lord. My girlfriend's simple words spoke volumes and restored a basic lesson I had forgotten: *"We thank you Father for all that we have, for all that we have comes from Thee."*

In the spring, Frank and I love the nursery's kaleidoscopic display of blossoms. Meandering through the lathe house, we scoop up luxuriant little plants. Tucking them into flats, we offer them a home in return for the showy production they provide in our landscape. Yet, sadly, their vivid colors, which feed our famished senses after winter's dreariness, are only temporary; their brilliance lasts but a few months.

When Frank was about ten years old, his mother offered him a small area in her garden where he planted and lovingly cared for nasturtiums throughout the summer. When fall appeared and the nasturtiums faded, Frank's mother had to explain that annuals endure merely a season. Determined to take on nature, Frank transplanted the flowers into a box on the back porch, hoping to prolong their beauty. Much to his dismay, nature's course ended their little lives, but not without teaching Frank an important lesson:

CHAPTER
37
Timeless Treasures

ordinary, earthly treasures will never offer lasting pleasure.

Occasionally God tempers my enjoyment of ordinary treasures by reminding me that material wealth is susceptible to destruction and any joy contributed to my life here on earth will one day pass away. That's what He did with my Queen Anne furniture.

About the time Frank and I finally had the financial wherewithal to purchase some fine Queen Anne furniture, we also decided to add a fluffy, white Great Pyrenees puppy to our family. The beautiful cherry furniture brought us great pleasure, as did our adorable puppy, Reuben. What could possibly shatter this ideal!

One day while vacuuming I was horrified to discover deep teeth marks in the legs of my cherished wing chairs. I couldn't believe my eyes! Surely the sweet, bundle of fur that delightfully nuzzled our necks

with his wet little doggy nose wouldn't do such a thing! I had never found a shredded sock, not even a shoe with a hole in the sole! But though the disfiguring evidence was merely circumstantial, I had to rule Reuben the guilty party.

I have never replaced the scarred chair legs. Instead, I allow the deep scratches to remind me that ordinary treasures *are* perishable; they cannot offer enduring enjoyment. The bright spring flowers come and go with the passing seasons, our furniture has since accumulated additional mars and scratches, even our "puppy" has aged and his 148-pound frame is resting from a second knee surgery. The distinct pleasure each

> *The man who has God for his treasure has all things in One. Many ordinary treasures may be denied him, or if he is allowed to have them, the enjoyment of them will be so tempered that they will never be necessary to his happiness.*
>
> A. W. TOZER

> *We do not look at the things which are seen, but at the things which are not seen. For the things which are seen are temporary, but the things which are not seen are eternal.*
>
> 2 CORINTHIANS 4:18

earthly thing brings to our lives is temporal; the joy it affords lasts but a season.

Limitless joy, on the other hand, is found in God's immeasurable bounty. The pearls of wisdom that do endure the test of time lie hidden in God's Word. They are waiting our discovery. Deep abiding peace comes when we apply God's principles to our lives; and for those who accept Christ's redeeming act of death on the cross, He extends the most valuable treasure of all—life eternal.

While ordinary treasures offer a seasonal return, the dividends collected on God's timeless treasures are abundant, unending, and indestructible. No one can take them from us.

Among my earliest memories, I am lovingly enfolded in my mother's arms in a warm woolen blanket. She is cradling my aching ear to a hot water bottle and singing softly:

Jesus loves me, this I know,
for the Bible tells me so.

Little ones to Him
belong,
they are weak but He is
strong.

My mother's life was, and still is, simple—complicated only by the six children to whom she has dedicated a lifetime of sharing the love of God and raising us on lessons from His Word. Through the example of their lives, my parents' taught me to love the Lord. My mother walked with me to the altar when I gave my life to Jesus.

Today the eyes I gazed into as a child continue to sparkle back from that same compassionate face, aged only slightly over the years. Her voice, still like that of a dove, melodiously cheers my heart. My mother's faithfulness to God and her devotion to her husband have inspired me to be the woman I am today.

Married in 1944, Mom prayerfully entrusted her marriage to the Lord as Dad piloted bombing raids over Northern Europe. After the war, they left the security of their Kentucky home for Northern Idaho and struggled financially while raising their family on a dry cleaner's income. Life was strenuous at times but, like the lunches Mom made, it was the little things that became daily reminders of God's faithfulness to her and her childhood sweetheart. I was touched that twenty-five years later, as a vice president for Merrill Lynch, Dad still carried Mom's lunches to work. Perhaps he treasured what they represented—the faithfulness of God and that of his devoted bride.

Alone now, Mom still sits at the

CHAPTER 38
Little Ones to Him Belong

kitchen table meditating on God's Word and praying for her family. And though Dad has passed on, his thoughts still unite with hers when she ponders the notes he penned in his Bible.

As a little girl I would sit in our apple tree and sing to Jesus the songs my mother had taught me. There, in that same tree, I decided I wanted to have a marriage like the one my parents had modeled. I dreamed of being devoted to a godly husband just as Mom was devoted to Dad.

On June 24, 1972, that little girl's dream came true. I consecrated myself to Frank as we openly dedicated our marriage to the Lord. I scripted Proverbs 3:6 in royal

The preciousness of God's Word is of great and intrinsic value, like silver refined to the highest degree; it has nothing in it to depreciate it. . . . All the saints in all ages have trusted it and so tried it, and it never deceived them nor frustrated their expectation. . . .

MATTHEW HENRY

For this is God, our God forever and ever; He will be our guide even to death.

PSALM 48:14

frosting across the top of our wedding cake. IN ALL THY WAYS ACKNOWLEDGE HIM, AND HE SHALL DIRECT THY PATHS.

"Little ones to Him belong," my mother sang in faith. *"They are weak but He is strong,"* was the truth she prayed I would learn.

In times of plenty and in times of want, I have carried on Mom's tradition. The lunches I now prepare for *my* childhood sweetheart have become *our* daily reminders of God's faithfulness. As long as these two "little ones" have faithfully acknowledged the Lord, He's been faithful to direct our path. And when we've been weak, He's been strong.

Since I began writing this book, four seasons have come and gone. Along our lane, yellow fawn-lilies, purple shooting-stars, and wake-robin trilliums have returned, unfurling their allegiance to spring. Once more the chill of winter has dissipated under the warmth of the sun's rays, but at this time of year one never knows what weather a day may bring. Thin wisps of clouds can, within hours, build into a thunderstorm and, depending on our temperatures, shower us with rain or snow or both!

Gazing through the arched windows above the cushioned seat in our loft, I see shafts of sunlight penetrating scattered clouds, while in the east a curtain of hail falls so thick it is impossible to see what lies in the distance. Sunlight, hail, snow, fog—each distinctly affects our lives and sweeps over us within a few short hours.

I reflect on the similarities between the unpredictable mountain weather and the twenty-five years of marriage that Frank and I have shared. Gloomy clouds and rainy storms certainly cast their shadows over our years, but they never held the power to totally obscure the light of our heavenly Father's countenance.

CHAPTER 39

Sunlight Through the Seasons

"You saw how the LORD your God carried you, as a man carries his son, in all the way that you went until you came to this place" (Deut. 1:31). This favorite Scripture has become a reminder to us of God's faithfulness in carrying us all the way that we have come. Memories of the early struggles when we were learning to trust God upon the tempestuous Sea of Life are eclipsed by reflections of a warm, spring-like season when apple blossoms unfolded like the love between us. Brisk winds have blown to test the strength that unites us, but the deep devotion born in that season of love holds us secure.

Our faith in the '80s endured years of

Yet as the sun on summer days gladdens us with beams more warm and bright than at other times, and as rivers are at certain seasons swollen by the rain, and as the atmosphere itself is sometimes fraught with more fresh, more bracing, or more balmy influences than heretofore, so is it with the mercy of God; it hath its golden hours; its days of overflow, when the Lord magnifieth His grace before the sons of men.

CHARLES SPURGEON
EVENING AND MORNING

drought when our future and hope lay in nothing more than the grace of God to provide for our needs. After burning out of the ministry, in what seemed a desolate period, God sent warm showers of compassion to revive our hearts. Breathing new life into our weary souls, He opened the windows of heaven and rained a new season upon us—the one we find ourselves in now.

Again I glance out my window and feel dispirited by the curtain of hail that still obscures the eastern valley. But my melancholy is soon dispelled by the approach of a sunny sky that is pushing the storm on. Jesus said, "I am the light of the world." Just as we know at midnight that the sun is going to rise in glistening rays tomorrow, so in the dark seasons of life we can rest assured that the light of God's countenance will brighten our way.

As comfort from above shines through each season, so the age-old promise continues: As surely as a man carries his son, so the Lord has borne us in all the way we've come—and He will carry us into tomorrow.

The LORD will guide you continually, and satisfy your soul in drought, and strengthen your bones; you shall be like a watered garden, and like a spring of water, whose waters do not fail.

ISAIAH 58:11

"Each new season holds
a unique lesson that,
when fabricated into our lives,
brings God's purpose,
His enrichment,
and His character."

Barb